"Alan and Lance offer a theory of the everyday for those who know that history is made in the present. . . . I hope they start a revolution."

—from the foreword by Erwin Raphael McManus,
author of *Wide Awake*

"Finally, a book that takes all the missional theory and turns it into practical reality for the average person. I can't think of a more important topic for followers of Jesus everywhere to be learning and living out."

—Dan Kimball, author of *They Like Jesus but Not the Church*

"The missional church movement doesn't focus on *doing* church better; it is about *being* church better in the world, where the mission of God is under way. God already has his people deployed in every domain of culture, so the challenge is releasing the church to be the church where it already *is. Right Here, Right Now* is a powerful new resource for this strategy. It is both inspirational and instructional for serious Jesus-followers who understand church as a verb."

—Reggie McNeal, author of *The Present Future and Missional Renaissance*

"In *Right Here, Right Now*, my friends Alan Hirsch and Lance Ford help us raise up a movement of people on mission. For too long, missional church writings have focused on pastors and neglected people. Alan and Lance help us involve all God's people in God's mission."

—Ed Stetzer, president of LifeWay Research

"Alan Hirsch and Lance Ford help us to see our role as missionaries in the twenty-first century in their outstanding book *Right Here, Right Now*. You will never again see yourself as just another average Christian. Alan and Lance help us see how every one of us can play a role in God's mission here and now."

—Dave Ferguson, lead pastor, Community Christian Church;
movement leader, NewThing

"Although Alan and Lance have influenced leaders of the highest calling, this book is for the peasants. You, me, and your friends . . .

maybe every Christian who wants Jesus to wink at them, give them the thumbs up, and say, 'Now that's how I wanted you to live!'"

—Hugh Halter, author of *AND*, *The Tangible Kingdom*, and *TK Primer*

"With this book, the writing on the missional church has gone from QED (*Quod Erat Demonstrandum*—'which was to be demonstrated') to QEF (*Quod Erat Faciendum*—'which was to be done'). Hirsch and Ford believe that we've 'demonstrated' enough. It's now time for 'doing.' This book shows how to be missional 'Right Here, Right Now.'"

—Leonard Sweet, professor, Drew Theological School, George Fox University

"If you are looking for a compass to navigate your neighborhood toward the gospel, this book will point you in the right direction."

—Frank Viola, author of *From Eternity to Here* and *Reimagining Church*

"Most Christian leaders have discovered the great depth of learning that my friend Alan Hirsch has brought to the American church. I am glad that you now have the opportunity to learn from my friend Lance Ford as well. These are voices that are equipping a missional church to be prepared for the future, right here, right now."

—Neil Cole, director of Church Multiplication Associates; author of *Organic Church* and *Organic Leadership*

"In *Right Here, Right Now*, Alan Hirsch and Lance Ford challenge us to live as agents of God's kingdom in every possible arena of our lives. A compelling read for everyone who longs to see authentic discipleship transform our world."

—Felecity Dale, House2House Ministries; author of *An Army of Ordinary People*

"We have a saying in Idaho where hunting is a vital part of our livelihood and culture: 'If you're going to shoot a flying duck, you have to lead it.' As a Christian leader who passionately longs to be effective in ministering the gospel in a rapidly changing world, I am desperate to grasp a prophetic understanding of where our culture is headed. In the book *Right Here, Right Now*, Alan Hirsch and Lance Ford not only lead the cultural duck, but provide insightful, precise vision for church leaders to be ready to pull the trigger—positioned to make impact."

—Tri Robinson, author of *Rooted in Good Soil: Cultivating and Sustaining Authentic Discipleship*; senior pastor, Vineyard Christian Fellowship, Boise, Idaho

"In this world where social responsibility and connectedness are coming together, people are going to volunteer and serve one another—regardless of faith or no faith. Volunteer statistics for our nation and the world for that matter are at an all-time high. The question is, why do we do it and what is our goal and the outcome that we see coming from it? Depending on how we answer that question, our approach is determined. What does it mean for a follower of Jesus to serve others? What are the implications? Why do we do it? Lance and Alan answer these questions and more for everyday followers of Jesus. Enough talk among the pastors and church leaders, enough focus on building and growing and reinventing the church. This mission and calling is for all of us. This book pushes the conversation in a healthy theological and practical way in that direction."

—Bob Roberts Jr., senior pastor, NorthWood Church; author of *Realtime Connections: Using Your Job to Connect with God's Global Work*

.

# RIGHT **HERE**
# RIGHT **NOW**

Embracing the Missional Life

The Shapevine Series

*Organic Leadership*
Neil Cole

*Untamed*
Alan Hirsch and Debra Hirsch

*Rooted in Good Soil*
Tri Robinson

*Right Here, Right Now*
Alan Hirsch and Lance Ford

Other Books by Alan Hirsch

*The Forgotten Ways: Reactivating the Missional Church*
*The Forgotten Ways Handbook: A Practical Guide for
Developing Missional Churches*

# RIGHT HERE RIGHT NOW

## EVERYDAY MISSION FOR EVERYDAY PEOPLE

## ALAN HIRSCH
## LANCE FORD

BakerBooks

a division of Baker Publishing Group
Grand Rapids, Michigan

© 2011 by Alan Hirsch and Lance Ford

Published by Baker Books
a division of Baker Publishing Group
P.O. Box 6287, Grand Rapids, MI 49516-6287
www.bakerbooks.com

Printed in the United States of America

Library of Congress Cataloging-in-Publication Data
Hirsch, Alan, 1969–
    Right here, right now : everyday mission for everyday people / Alan Hirsch and Lance Ford.
       p.   cm. — (Shapevine)
    Includes bibliographical references.
    ISBN 978-0-8010-7223-9 (pbk.)
    1. Missions—Theory. 2. Evangelistic work. 3. Mission of the church. I. Ford, Lance, 1959– II. Title. III. Title: Everyday mission for everyday people.
    BV2063.H53 2011
    266.001—dc22
                                                      2010034306

11  12  13  14  15  16  17      7  6  5  4  3  2  1

Dedicated to our amazing Lord Jesus—God's sent One who has redeemed us and shown us the right way to live. Also to all those who have provided me with wonderful living examples of what it means to engage incarnationally *right here, right now*—especially John Jensen, Lindy Croucher, Darryn Altclass, Hugh Halter, and of course the magnificent Debra Hirsch.

Alan Hirsch

《《 》》

Dedicated to my father, Kenneth Ford—whom I will always remember as *Daddy*. And to my literal dream girl and life partner, Sherri, whose tireless devotion and encouragement inspires and fuels me every day.

Lance Ford

Online Resources for
Individual & Group Study

>>> videos for each chapter
>>> participant guides

righthererightnowbook.com

# CONTENTS

# FOREWORD

Every generation, I suppose, has a sense of its own uniqueness. Much of this is formed in response to the culture and values of the previous generation. Much of what we create is either an expression or reaction to the world given us by our ancestors.

This is nowhere more evident than in the modern Western church where much of its innovation and change has been a reaction to the growing irrelevance of the established church. We have seen a seismic shift away from the polarizing lines of denominations and a shift from distinctions based on secondary theological differences.

At the same time this has not brought a greater unity or collaboration. It has resulted in a search for new anchors and metaphors from which to draw our identity. We are more fragmented and divided than ever.

The lines are getting narrower. It has become even more "us" verses "them." We are in a period where we are more defined by what we are against than what we are for.

One of the peculiar trends I have seen over the past twenty years is the demarcation of the church based less on theology and more on methodology. Both have always been critical, but the order has changed. We seem to be arguing less on interpretations of the Scriptures and more on two fronts— epistemology and methodology.

There is a fragmenting line around truth: "What is its source?" "What can be known?" "What is our authority?" and even and especially "Is the Bible relevant and trustworthy?"

My experience is that a person's confession or convictions has little to do with how they are categorized concerning these issues. We live in a time where our methodology defines our relationship to orthodoxy. Those formed by modernity seem to be either unwilling or incapable of understanding the difference. Those informed by postmodernity seem determined to be identified by what they don't know and what they are against.

Which leads me to why I am writing this foreword. As I travel the world and have interactions with those of us who are familiar with the heated conversations about the church, I am often asked which camp we fall into. Are we a "missional" church or an "attractional" church? Are we "emergent" or "emerging"? If we refuse to embrace these categories or submit to them, those who ask choose one for us.

Yet the everyday person of faith isn't asking these questions. They are irrelevant to them. All they want to know is whether the church can help them as they struggle to follow Christ and live out their faith in the real world. We are answering questions they are not asking. Worse, we are leaving their most important questions unattended.

What we need is to help people right here, right now! What we need is an everyday mission for everyday people. Alan Hirsch and Lance Ford are not megachurch pastors or crusade evangelists; they are guys who love God and want their lives to count. They want to serve as guides for everyday people.

That's why I like what they are trying to do. They are trying to get to ground zero and help those in the trenches. Nothing glitzy. Nothing particularly spectacular. Just real life. Alan and Lance offer a theory of the everyday for those who know that history is made in the present.

*Right Here, Right Now: Everyday Mission for Everyday People.* Alan and Lance: I hope you start a revolution.

erwin raphael mcmanus

# ABOUT THE SHAPEVINE
# MISSIONAL SERIES

The key purpose of Shapevine the organization is to bring the various elements of missional Christianity—namely, church planting movements, urban mission, the emerging church, the missional church movement, the organic/simple church, and marketplace ministries—into meaningful dialogue around the truly big ideas of our time. Consistent with this purpose, the Shapevine Missional Series in partnership with Baker Books seeks to bring innovative thinking to the missional issues of church planting, mission, evangelism, social justice, and anything in between.

We seek to publish both established authors as well as others who have significant things to contribute but have operated largely under the radar.

The series will focus on three distinctive areas:

- Living—Practical Missional Orthopraxy
  Orthopraxy is what makes orthodoxy worth having. We yearn for the experience and continual flow of living out the gospel message in our day-to-day lives for the sake

of others. The stories and ideas in the Shapevine Missional Series are aimed at providing practical handles and means to wrap our readers' minds around the idea of living as the people of God, sent into the world with the Spirit and impulse of Jesus himself.

- **Learning—Solid Missional Orthodoxy**
  Jesus both lived and proclaimed a theology of a missional God. His was and is a message of mercy, justice, and goodness toward others. It was this message that erupted into the greatest movement in the history of humankind. The same God who sent his only Son now sends those who follow his Son, in the same manner and with the same message. This is at the heart of a missional theology.

- **Leading—Tools for Missional Leadership**
  Our aim is for the books in this series to serve as tools for pastors, organizational leaders, and church members throughout the world to equip themselves and others as they travel the path of faithfulness in the missional life.

As a global interactive forum, Shapevine allows anyone to both learn and contribute at whatever level suits. To learn more, go to www.shapevine.com or contact us at info@ shapevine.com.

Alan Hirsch and Lance Ford

# SERIES EDITOR'S PREFACE

There is little doubt something *fundamental* is going on when it comes to our thinking about church in relation to the contexts in which we find ourselves. *Right Here, Right Now* is a book for these times. Its publication coincides with a number of significant books, events, and manifestos that highlight the paradigm shift taking place in our day—what is generally called the missional church movement.

But the truth is that most of these defining events and texts remain largely a church leadership affair—and a pretty highfalutin one at that. The weighty ideas of the missional church movement and, beyond this, the sheer power it represents for the wholesale renewal of Christianity in our time and place remains largely incomprehensible to the masses of people who don't have the time and training to engage these world-changing ideas at the more technical level.

*Right Here, Right Now* is a book designed to remedy this situation and thereby make missional church what it should be: a movement of the whole people of God in every sphere and domain of society. While Lance and I only glance at issues relating specifically to church and church planting here, we are dedicated to helping the average believer become an effective agent of the King wherever they might find themselves. Without meaning this in any derogatory sense, this is in effect a missionality-for-dummies type book—missionality for anyone, anywhere, and anytime. Hopefully you will find it accessible, challenging, intriguing, and motivational all at once.

This fits well with what the Baker-Shapevine series seeks to do: to provide a forum for all of God's redeemed people to engage with world-changing ideas. It complements our previous publications by authors Neil Cole (*Organic Leadership*), Debra and Alan Hirsch (*Untamed*), and Tri Robinson (*Rooted in Good Soil*)—all accessible, missional, and challenging reads.

And it is with this sense of trying to serve the cause of Jesus and his church that we entrust this book to your critical engagement.

Alan Hirsch
Shapevine series editor

# INTRODUCTION

Just over a decade ago the seminal, but very technical, work of the Gospel and Our Culture Network (GOCN.org) arrived on the scene and began to give language for what our most perceptive church leaders had either been thinking or sensing for sometime prior to that. In the time since *Missional Church* was published, the word *missional* has become the veritable belle of the ball: a Google search yields about two and a half million results in less than a second. But belles can be such voguish creatures, destined to fade away. Will it be the same with the term *missional?* Well, not on our shift! Not if we can help it.

We do not believe, as some have suggested, that missional is a fad. We believe it touches on the very nature of Christianity and is therefore foundational to the message of Jesus. But because of the largeness of the concept, the word *missional* does not easily submit to definitions; certainly it is not a technique or a church growth system or tool.

For followers of Jesus, *missional* shapes our discipleship, defines our ministry, describes our mission, and points to the very purpose of his church. It's a term that comes from the inside of God and from deep within the nature of the church that Jesus built.

Our hope for this book is that it will serve as a tool and resource, whether you are a pastor or church planter or simply a follower of Jesus trying to get it right in love and obedience to our Lord. This book is written to equip all believers and to serve as a guide in the journey of living as salt and light in the name of Jesus Christ, regardless of situation, vocation, or location. It is to take the rather academic concept of *missional* and make it accessible to the whole body of Christ. We believe it belongs to the whole church and must somehow be factored into the equation of discipleship, spirituality, and church at every level of our experience if we are going to be the people God has made us to be.

Through engaging with thousands of pastors, church planters, and church leaders across North America, Europe, and Australia, we are consistently confronted with questions about how to engage missionally—in urban, rural, or suburban contexts. Misunderstanding and stereotypes abound. Many suburban folk misconstrue missional engagement as something that takes place primarily in poor city central or in exploited parts of the world. Others hold the view that it involves church outreach/evangelism in the neighborhood or churchwide evangelistic efforts abroad. Some see missional as simply planting new churches, yet others see it as involving social justice activism and living in radical communities among the poor and marginalized.

The truth is, all of these are aspects of missional engagement, but on their own, separated from the whole, they form only part of the equation. And it is the whole we must see to fully understand what we are dealing with. Missionality involves every believer who seeks to follow Jesus authentically *right here, right now*. It is linked to discipleship, and discipleship is a function of the church, which is connected to the lordship of Jesus. The lordship of Jesus involves every one of us as a representative of the King in every sphere and domain of society. That's what we are trying to encourage: missional Christianity—a spunky, high-impact, life-oriented, world-transforming, joyous, living for Jesus our King. An outward-focused, kingdom-oriented discipleship that changes our world.

## Living the Adjective

So we have set our aim here to help Christians see the kingdom opportunities that exist on the pathways of their daily routines and lifestyle patterns and to *live* missionally more than simply *do* mission activities. We want to take this adjective, *missional*, and make it a living reality in the lives of Christians everywhere. All Christians, whether suburban or urban, blue collar or white collar, have *already* been *sent* by God on a mission and they have tremendous kingdom potential in the here and now of their current situations. God is already there at work in our neighborhoods, workplaces, amusement parks, schools, movie theatres, pubs, or wherever, and we must learn again what it means to courageously join him in his mission of redeeming his world. Like we say in our subtitle, we want to awaken a spicy missional moxie, not just in so-called professional Christians and clergy, but *in everyone*.

The intention of this book is not simply to decry the failures of the Western church or to paint a Mayberryesque vision of some sort of utopia. Simply adding quarterly block parties or participating in urban plunges is not enough to be *missional*—although, as we shall see, they certainly can be part of it. What we are proposing goes deeper and should hopefully result in a reformation of the way we actually live our lives as Jesus followers. To do this we have to recast vision, play with paradigms, dream out loud, shout, coax, whisper. However we might achieve it, we don't want to leave you unchanged.

So we are going to play the part of missiological optometrists, fitting you with eyewear that helps you see a way of living faithfully to God's mission in the world, *right here, right now*. And we want to help you connect with the sheer joy of living with that little adjective firmly in its place—a missional (which is to say *authentic*, indeed *biblical*) form of Christianity.

## How We Have Written This Book

You will soon find this is a little different from most co-authored books. The contents of the book are sandwiched between a *briefing* chapter ("Right Here") in the beginning and a *debriefing* chapter ("Right Now") at the end, both written by Alan. These are designed to provide a framework for new thinking and acting. The middle sections are written by Lance, but Alan inserts himself into the conversation all along the way, like a resident heckler or a built-in commentator of sorts, whose ideas cajole us to think more deeply about things being discussed. Our writing process has included countless hours discussing these chapters, and Lance has focused on bringing Alan's perspectives to the contents. The remarks in the Just Sayin' columns therefore are designed to provide further prompts and boosts to the story that is woven around it. We think this is both a playful and helpful literary device, but it also allows us to speak with our own voices. Alan, for reasons known only to God, is the more technical and theologically geeky, and will therefore role-play the resident don throughout the book. Lance, on the other hand, will be the folksier, easygoing American interpreter and storyteller, playfully suggesting ways in which we can integrate these ideas into our everyday lives. Between the two of us, we hope you will hear something of the Word of God to our time.

## Some Other Splinters for Your Mind

Three books will be important here, and they will be referred to throughout these pages. The first one, *Untamed*,[1] is on the nature of missional discipleship and is utterly foundational to the issue of what it means to be a missional Christian right here, right now. We recommend you consider reading this book as a backup to the one in your hand now. For foundational approaches to incarnational mission in the West, we recommend *The Shaping of Things to Come* as the backup text.[2] Although a harder read, many of the ideas in this book find their origin there. And thirdly, for applying missionality throughout the church and church organizations, we suggest reading *The Forgotten Ways Handbook*.[3] This is an intensely practical reworking of the more theoretical *The Forgotten Ways*[4] (if, however, you want to really dig in to the ideas, go there). You might also look into *ReJesus: A Wild Messiah for a Missional Church*,[5] a book written to take us all back to Jesus to rediscover what it's all about in the first place.

The other books that help us reframe the way we engage our worlds are Hugh Halter and Matt Smay's *The Tangible Kingdom: Creating Incarnational Community*, which has the associated *Tangible Kingdom Primer*. These are top-rate tools that help churches becoming incarnational (as the subtitle suggests) with a focus primarily on the *communal* side of the equation.[6] Michael Frost's *Exiles*[7] and Neil Cole's *Search and Rescue* and *Organic Church* are excellent, highly accessible works on missional discipleship and church. Some older, more evangelistically inclined books are Shamy and Petersen's *The Insider* and Randy Frazee's *The Connecting Church*. And a serious classic is Roland Allen's *Missionary Methods: St. Paul's or Ours?* Books by Reggie McNeal are also gems, especially *Missional Renaissance*. All of these are designed to reframe the way we see Christianity and reorient us to becoming a missional church again in our time.

For accessible, context-based training, we suggest the various offerings of Shapevine (shapevine.com), Forge (forgeamerica.org, forgecanada.ca, forge.org.au), and Missio (missio.us); Church 3.0 in Alabama (3mlt.com); and in the UK we suggest Together in Mission (togetherinmission. co.uk).

Anyhow, enough about books and training, let's get to the real thing—living the message in a way that brings Jesus into the imagination and experience of people who would never normally get access to him through our current means. We have a great opportunity in our day through our decisions and deeds to maximize impact in ways we never dreamed of before. If ever there was a time to get our act together, it is now. So, here's to faithfulness, authenticity, and loving Jesus in ways he deserves.

> When we get out of the glass bottles of our ego,
> and when we escape like squirrels turning in the
> cages of our personality
> and get into the forests again,
> we shall shiver with cold and fright
> but things will happen to us
> so that we don't know ourselves.
>
> Cool, unlying life will rush in,
> and passion will make our bodies taut with power,
> we shall stamp our feet with new power
> and old things will fall down,
> we shall laugh, and institutions will curl up like
> burnt paper.
>
> — D. H. Lawrence

BRIEFING

RIGHT HERE

# FRAMEWORKS FOR MISSIONAL CHRISTIANITY

## ALAN HIRSCH

You are here because you know something. What you
know you can't explain but you feel it. You felt it your
entire life. There is something wrong with the world but
you don't know what it is. But it's there like a splinter
in your mind.

—Morpheus to Neo,
*The Matrix*

You can no longer remain unconscious where you slept
before; one way or another, you are creating your future.
Wake up before you find that the devils within you have
done the creating.

—Stephen L. Talbot,
*The Future Does Not Compute*

In many ways this book is all about connecting ourselves,
not with a trendy new movement, but by reconnecting the
current Christian church with the power of the original one.

It is one of my deepest held beliefs that *all* of Jesus' people contain the potential for world transformation in them. Our problem is not that we don't have the potential, but rather that we have forgotten how to access these potentials because we have been so deeply scripted to think of ourselves through more domesticated, non-missional manifestations of Christianity. We have been so programmed out of our callings that it is generally hard for us to think and act differently than what we have for hundreds of years and not to persecute people who try to trailblaze alternative ways. But we have now come (at last!) to the point where we can recognize that the decline of Christianity in the West, and now in America, is directly related to the way we have done things to this point. The search for alternatives has just heated up. Aslan is on the move again and it's time to get unplugged, reframed, rescripted, and recommissioned to be the people Jesus designed us to be.

If this was said another way, I would suggest we are *perfectly designed to achieve what we are currently achieving.* If Christianity is in decline, at least part of the issue goes to the contemporary way we live out faith in a watching world. But this is not what Jesus intended. The church that Jesus designed is made for impact—and massive, highly transformative impact at that. Wasn't it Jesus who said, "I will build My church, and the gates of Hades shall not prevail against it" (Matt. 16:18 NKJV). Hang on! Jesus says that the gates of hell don't prevail against us! It is we as God's people who are on the advance here, not hell! Contrary to many of the images of church as a defensive fortress suffering the terrible, relentless onslaughts of hell, the movement that Jesus set in motion is designed to be an advancing, untamed, and untamable revolutionary force created to transform the world. And make no mistake—there is in Jesus' words here a real sense of inevitability about the eventual triumph of the gospel. If we are not somehow part of this, then there is something wrong in the prevailing designs and they must change.

Reading this (definitely but necessarily too big) chapter is going to feel like drinking from a fire hydrant, because it summarizes, hopefully in highly accessible ways, ideas that have been formulated and developed in much more detail elsewhere. But this is my (Alan's) "formal briefing," or conceptual framing, for a missionality that can be lived out right here, right now, by everyone. And this, my friends, takes some reframing . . . some redesigning of the way we go about being God's people. The concepts offered here *will* be made much clearer through the use of story and examples of everyday Christians and churches throughout the rest of the book. But we have to clarify what we are talking about in the first place, so this thorough briefing should be treated as the point of reference and returned to when necessary.

## Move It

Let's start this journey to what we call "missionality" with a big statement that sets the tone for all that will follow: I believe with all my heart that the future of Christianity in the West is somehow bound up with the idea of becoming a *people movement* again. Somehow and in some way, we need to loosen up and learn how to reactivate the massive potentials that lie rather dormant within Jesus' people if we are going to make a difference to our world.

It is only when the people of God as a whole are activated in a movement that real world transformation takes place. And so understanding the nature of people movements is essential. When we look at high-impact movements in the Bible and history, we can see that there are two basic elements of a missional movement that can change the world. If one is missing, then the other will not be able to sustain, let alone reach, exponential impact.

One dimension relates to what I call the *apostolic mission* (AM), which involves the church or communal side of the movement—the distinctly *ecclesial* wing. It is critical for the *ecclesia* (the church) to multiply and cross cultural boundaries for a movement to take place. This is usually spearheaded by people whose primary work is to direct and focus Jesus' people and organize groups, networks, and hubs into apostolic networks that expand exponentially. In other words, people committed to ministry with, and through, the church as an organized community. AM is therefore normally expressed through church planting and organized mission to the poor or cross-culturally. Most of the people reading this book will probably not fit into this category.

The other equally vital (and much harder to galvanize) aspect is what I call the *mission of the whole people of God* (MPOG), which involves activating the whole people of God and empowering every believer to be active agents of God's kingdom in every sphere of life. Everyone in this movement, and not just the so-called religious professionals, must be activated and thus play a vital role in extending the mission of Jesus' church. The people involved in this dimension of people movements are those committed to full-time ministry *outside* of the church community . . . but it is still full-time ministry. In fact, this false distinction in what constitutes ministry is one of the major hurdles we have to overcome if we are going to activate as Jesus' people.

And while most of my writings have focused on the apostolic mission side of the equation, it is absolutely critical that we as the whole people of God are activated. If missional

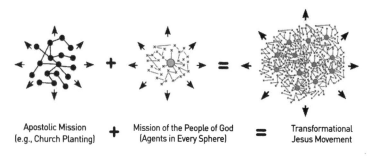

| Apostolic Mission (e.g., Church Planting) | + | Mission of the People of God (Agents in Every Sphere) | = | Transformational Jesus Movement |

church remains solely in the domain of leaders and clergy, then it is doubtful we will have any lasting missional impact in the long term. It's going to take both *missional church plus missional disciples to make a missional movement.*

### Conversion Is Commission

You *are* the church before you *do* church. If we take Jesus at his word when he says, "As the Father has sent me, I am sending you" (John 20:21), then we realize that our being "sent" (Latin: *missio*) is the basis of our "doing" church and not the other way around. What is more, this applies to every disciple and not just to the so-called clergy (the *called ones*). We are all called into the kingdom and into living our life under orders. What we normally infer by the word *church* limits what the Bible means by it. Church is not simply a building or a formal community meeting, it is who we *are*—a people who have been formed out of a direct encounter with God in Jesus Christ. If this is true, then general practice in church planting, which simply amounts to "service planting," actually activates only one side of the movement equation—namely, apostolic mission—but it leaves the MPOG undervalued and almost totally passive and unengaged. This is a fatal error.

### The Worldwide Message Tribe

We are a unique people formed by the life-changing message of the gospel of Jesus Christ—in effect, a worldwide message tribe. But if we are recipients of a pay-it-forward type message, one that must be passed on, then that makes us all messengers! Every believer is therefore a messenger . . . and in the terms of this book, a *missionary*. And Christianity itself is an intrinsically *missional* faith. Even the newest believer seems to understand the universality of the gospel message; they rightly intuit that because it is "good news," it is *meant* to be passed on, and that somehow to sit on the message is to fail in our obligations to Jesus and his cause.

This is how missional movements grow—through a group of people who have been changed by Jesus and are willing to put themselves on the line for his cause. And the cause cannot be limited to evangelism, as if simply telling someone about the saving events of Jesus' life and death fulfills our missional obligations. Rather it is about living the gospel in such a way that people are drawn into the direct influence (lordship) of Jesus through our lives. It is about living according to a distinct vision of society built on God's dreams and desires—not ours. In other words, as Rick Warren wryly says, it's not all about you; rather it is about the kingdom (or rule) of God over all creation. It encompasses everything in human experience—from culture, race, economics, church, entertainment, family, and everything in between. A missional movement must apply the gospel to all spheres of life (business, family, art, education, science, politics, etc.)—it cannot be limited simply to "coming to church" or participating in building-based programs.

The reality is that it doesn't take millions of admirers to start a movement that can change the world (in fact, that might be problematic). What *is* needed is a few people who have been personally transformed and are committed enough to the cause to be willing to in some way or another put their lives in the service of extending it into every domain of life. It is the personal commitment levels that make all the difference—that's why Jesus was willing to invest most of his time in "the Twelve" and by extension in "the seventy." Once he had seeded the essence of his message into his disciples, he could then focus on his upcoming death and resurrection (see Matt. 16:13–21), leaving behind a small band of people who did go on to change the world with it. And this is why being an authentic disciple is so important to his mission. As I say in *The Forgotten Ways*, embodiment (the capacity to actually integrate and live out the teachings and message of Jesus) is critical to transmission (the capacity to transfer the message through relationships).[1]

And in some ways, this is all that is still needed today—real disciples. Jesus will do the necessary transforming; the part we play is to be willing to be used in that process of living the message and getting it out into our worlds. All it needed was people who were willing to be an authentic message tribe. Seth Godin, pop movements guru, rightly notes that creating a highly dedicated and closely knit tribe usually leads to much more impact than simply trying to make a tribe bigger. "Beyond public relations and awareness related benefits, measuring the breadth of spread of an idea is not as important as looking at the depth of commitment and interaction of true fans, who end up being the people who recruit most new members."[2]

In short, what is needed from us is the willingness to move with the Move of God that is the gospel. We suggest that there are a number of movements needed on our behalf if we are indeed going to partake of the movement that Jesus started. We have to be willing to

- move *out* (into missional engagement),
- move *in* (burrowing down into the culture),
- move *alongside* (engaging in genuine friendships and relational networks), and
- move *from* (challenging the dehumanizing and sinful aspects of our culture).

## Move Out (Mission)

So the first movement of mission required of us is the willingness to move out—to simply go to the people, wherever that might be. Movement by defintion suggests some form of motion, some type of action: it might not be far, but the obligation is on us to go to them, not them to us.

### The Mission Has a Church

We have already mentioned that we are people who live under an obligation to extend the mission and meaning of

Jesus into our world. The way I framed this in *The Forgotten Ways* was to say that it is not so much that the church has a mission but that the mission has a church. What this meant is that we really are the result of God's missionary activity in the world: God sends (*missio*) his Son into the world. Another way of saying this is that God is the Sending God and the Son is the Sent One. The Father and Son in turn "send" the Spirit into the world (so it turns out that the Spirit is a missionary too). And what is more, Jesus says that as the Father sent him, so he sends and commissions each of us as fully empowered missional agents of the King (John 17:18; 20:21; Matt. 28:19).

### Any Time, Any Place

Every Christian is a missionary and we are called to live out our commitment to Jesus' lordship in every sphere and domain of life. Church life, as we normally conceive it, is only one dimension of life and all of us inhabit many other realms that make up our lives. What marks Christianity as distinct is that it is truly a people movement: every believer (and not just some presumed religious elite) is an agent of the kingdom and is called to bring God's influence into all the realms of human existence. Just look to our New Testament for this! Because the Holy Spirit lives in us, and we are all bearers of the gospel message, we are all agents of the King right here, right now, and at any time and in any place.

### Build a Bridge and Get Over It

My wife Deb has this wonderfully humbling thing to say about men and missional church. She says that we men tend to talk and write about it while most women just tend to do it. She follows up with a quick second blow by saying "After all is said and done, it's all about learning to love other people as Jesus did, isn't it?" And even though I find this argument exasperating, I really have to agree.

## Learning the art of the small

1. One person can make an impact.
2. Concentrate your efforts on smaller and smaller areas. When your efforts are diffused over a wide area, they won't have much of an impact. So focus on smaller areas, and your efforts will be felt more fully. It could take time for change to happen, but keep that focus narrow.
3. Try to find an area that will cause a tipping point. You'll have the biggest impact if you can change something that will in itself cause further changes—the rock that causes the avalanche. This isn't an easy thing, to find that pressure point, that spot that will cause everything else to change. It takes practice and experience and luck and persistence, but it can be found.
4. Don't try to beat an ocean. You'll lose. Instead, focus on small changes that will spread.[3]

For most of us, what will be required to engage in missional Christianity is to simply reach out beyond our fears and ignorance of others, to overcome our middle-class penchant for safety, to take a risk and get involved in what God is already doing in our cities and neighborhoods. It's not a science really, although as we will see, there are sometimes tricky cultural elements to deal with. It is all about love. Just read 1 John again to remind yourself of this.

### Use What's in Your Hand

One of the most significant things to remember in getting missional is often the thing we most overlook. It's not all about starting grand programs and running big organizations. It is just doing what you do . . . for God. The basic elements of missionality are already present in your life. It might develop into an organization (e.g., Tom's Shoes, Laundry Love),[4] but it probably should not start there. In this book we will explore many ways we can simply use the basic constituents of life and make them an act of worship to God and service to his world. Sometimes simple gestures make all the difference. Don't be overwhelmed. Certainly, prepare yourself in prayer and study of the gospel and culture, but trust that God will use you as you are—he has always done so. You don't need a degree to be a very effective agent of the King. A saint is merely a person who makes it easier for others to believe in God. Mother Teresa (of all people!) once famously quipped, "I don't do big things. I do small things with big love." We are not required to do a great thing in life, but many, many small things, each done with love.

## Move In (Incarnation)

So we are called to be a missional (move out) people, and if we are willing to follow the missional Spirit, I venture to bet that we will end up in some rather unusual situations and places. And we don't mean just cross-cultural here: it might simply mean reaching over your fence, and beyond that into the local neighborhood. But don't be surprised if this is still a bit of a challenge to you. One of the things that has happened over the last decade or so is a massive cultural shift away from the Judeo-Christian heritage into a truly subcultural, multicultural experience . . . our neighborhoods have gone and changed on us.

To move deep into the culture is to take the idea of incarnational mission seriously. This in turn takes its cue from the fact that God took on human form and moved into our neighborhood, assumed the full reality of our humanity, identified with us, and spoke to us from within a common experience. Following his example, and in his cause, we take the same type of approach when it comes to mission.

### Going Tribal

Whether we like it or not, we live in a world that is culturally fragmented and fragmenting. The result of cultural disintegration is that people now choose to identify with various subcultural groups. Any modern city is now made up of literally thousands of different subcultures: from sports groups, hobby clubs, interest groups, to groups that gather around sexual preference (the gay community is always a big one in major cities throughout the West), to pubs, clubs, music groups, surfers, skaters . . . you name it!

Moving deep means that we choose to connect with, identify with, and belong to one or a few of these urban tribes. Don't try identifying with everyone within your reach—if this does not drive you mad, it certainly will exhaust you. Rather focus your efforts on meaningful connections with certain people and people groups. Go where they go, hang out where they hang out, do what they do. I have seen churches develop this in the strangest of normal places: along riverbanks with the waterskiing community, rave clubs, amateur drama theatres, online game communities. I know of one young mom who, instead of attending the local church's MOPS program, chose to adopt one of the many local non-Christian mothers groups. She was soon asked to lead it and her influence as a Christian was significantly magnified, more than if she had simply attended the local Christian version.

### St. Paul Goes to the Movies

A few years ago I ran and organized a conference called St. Paul Goes to the Movies. The idea was to help Christians lean how to share faith from within diverse cultural settings in Western contexts. My advice to all Christians is, in order to take missionality seriously, you have to take culture seriously. There is no dodging this aspect. You simply have to assume that, in Western contexts, all communication of the gospel, let alone church planting and mission, is now cross-cultural. Don't presume you really know what's going on. The reality is that most Christians don't really know what goes on in the lives of non-Christian people. Research indicates that the majority of Christians have no significant relationships with people beyond their church community. To move out (get missional), and to move in (get incarnational), this must change.

If you find yourself called to a certain urban tribe, whoever they might be, then it is critical that you take *their* culture—in effect, their meaning system—seriously. Go to movies with friends and talk about the themes. Read the books they are likely to read (there is good demographical information about lifestyle preferences and people groups around). Browse bookshops and magazine racks as to what people are talking about and interested in. If people see a movie more than once, make sure you see it and try to work out what it is they seemed to resonate with. Then you can get to see how the Good News relates to the issue.

The missional Christian makes the connections between people's existential issues and the gospel, as we shall see, but it does take some cultural savvy to make this happen well.

### Redeeming Your Hangout (Third Places, etc.)

Missionality right here, right now does not always require you to go to places and people you find so different and uncomfortable. In the principle of starting with what's already in your hand, make a list of the things you love to do. Odds are there are a whole lot of people who already do one of those things together, and if not, then there are probably people who would like to do that with others. Another approach is to list the vibrant social spaces in your area and simply adopt one and become a regular. Don't do this as some sort of lone missional ranger. How about a few of you take this on as a common mission.

Some popular interests include art forms, murals, beer brewing, cooking, cycling. A look at your local newspaper will reveal hundreds of such groups around. For example, I know of a group of believers who simply loved bush walking— trekking through the mountains and hills around Melbourne. Problem was, the only free day they had was Sunday, so they decided to make that their church. They would trek out into the bush, taking in the glories of God's creation and good comradeship along the way. At a certain point they would stop, have a meal and communion together, share around Scripture, take an offering, pray for people, and then continue bush walking for the rest of the day. About 40 percent of the group were non-Christians deeply interested in the mix of nature and spirituality that The Earth Club provided. The church that Jesus built doesn't need all the institutional paraphernalia that we have been scripted to think it does. You carry it with you everywhere you go.

### Speaking the Lingo (All Mission Is Cross-Cultural)

All missionaries must deal with language. To speak the lingo means to understand and adopt the language forms of the people we love and serve. We do so in order to represent Jesus meaningfully in the group itself. Tim Keller, one of the elder statesmen of the missional church world, encourages us to enter and retell the culture's stories with the gospel rather than the other way around.[5] For instance, in church circles there is a certain insider language—a common worldview that allows us to simply exhort Christianized people with little or no real engagement, listening, or persuasion. In a missional setting, communication should always assume the presence of skeptical people and should engage their stories, not simply talk the church's insider story and language. This requires that we are sensitive to story and language and how these inform identity and community.

> The older culture's story was to be a good person, a good father/mother, son/daughter, to live a decent, merciful, good life. Now the culture's story is—(a) to be free and self-created and authentic (theme of freedom from oppression), and (b) to make the world safe for everyone else to be the same (theme of inclusion of the "other"; justice). To "re-tell" means to show how only in Christ can we have freedom without slavery and embracing of the "other" without injustice.[6]

To listen to the culture's stories, we need to be attentive. Once again movies and art form will give us a good clue, because great art is a way in which people seek to express meaning. For instance, in what way do the movies *Revolutionary Road*, *The Matrix*, or *The Pursuit of Happyness* tell us about our culture's story and values? Test this; try asking people what their absolutely favorite movie is, and why this is so, and you will hear a lot about that person. This is a great way to try to understand and unlock people's culture code.

Watch Paul the missionary in Athens: he is very sensitive to their religion, poetry, and philosophy (Acts 17). In this context Paul exegetes the culture, allowing the biblical story to inform and guide him—but he starts with the culture and ends with the gospel. In Jerusalem it's a different story; he whips out his big black King James (or equivalent) and he begins with Scripture and proceeds to culture. The more and more America slips into the encroaching post-Christian experience, the more and more we are going to have to take an Athenian approach to engaging it. In a missional context, Christians must learn to behave like culturally tuned missionaries.

### Wired for God

One of the most basic assumptions of the incarnational missionary is to assume God is already involved in every person's life and is calling them to himself through his Son. Our mindset should not be the prevalent one of taking God with us wherever we might go. It must be, instead, that we join God in *his* mission.

This means that the missionary God has been active a long time in a person's life. Our primary job is to try to see where and how God has been working and to partner with him in bringing people to redemption in Jesus. Understanding that all humans are made in the image and likeness of God (Gen. 1:27), and in the deepest possible way made *for* God, we can assume that every human is motivated by spirituality and search for meaning. Even idolatry indicates that people are seeking to worship something beyond themselves. It is deformed spirituality to be sure, but it *is* spirituality nonetheless—and you can work with that. Recognize that behind many of the things not-yet-Christian people do lies a search for something else. C. S. Lewis once noted that all our vices are virtues gone wrong. If we take this as a clue, we can develop new missionary eyes to see what God is up to in people's lives.

Let's take a deeper look at this: consider Las Vegas, the consummate sinner's town. And it is that—a deeply broken place where people get really messed up. But we can put aside our moral misgivings and choose to look at the gambling dens with more missional eyes. We might ask, what is the person who is sitting at the slot machines *really* searching for? Perhaps it is the search for redemption but in the wrong place. It is the belief that to win the jackpot means to be changed and transformed into a new life. This search might also be driven by a now pathological need to take risks because life has lost its sense of real adventure.

We can literally work our way through any type of event or activity in this way:

| Event or activity | What is *really* being sought? | How the gospel addresses this issue |
| --- | --- | --- |
| Gambling | • Redemption by luck/money<br>• Need for risk<br>• Overcoming unhappiness | • Finding meaning in doing things<br>• Hope<br>• Call to live adventurously and risk lovingly as a disciple |
| Sports events | • A cause to belong to<br>• Transcendent experiences<br>• Community with team/fans | • A real cause that aims at changing the world<br>• Real transcendent experience<br>• Authentic community |
| Pubs | • Community<br>• A partner<br>• Overcoming loneliness<br>• Fun/chill time | • Real but loving community<br>• Highs without drugs<br>• Nonexploitative relationships<br>• Lasting joy |

| Event or activity | What is *really* being sought? | How the gospel addresses this issue |
|---|---|---|
| Drug-taking | • Ecstatic experiences<br>• Escaping from life<br>• Overcoming guilt and pain | • Encountering God<br>• Meaning and purpose<br>• Forgiveness and healing |
| Movies | • Hearing the stories and myths that shape life<br>• Suspension of disbelief<br>• Entertainment/escape<br>• "Feeling" again (laughing, crying, etc.) | • Connection with the Story that makes sense of our stories<br>• Reality, not fantasy<br>• Passion leading to compassion |

We can trust that because of the way God has designed us, in the end human beings are always searching (albeit in false and idolatrous ways) for real meaning, authentic relationships, to love and be loved in return.

One more dimension of this that must be mentioned is that all people have religious experiences. It is false to say that only Christians can experience God. Anyone looking at a sunset can experience an in-breaking of God-awareness. In *The Color Purple*, Celia recalls a time as a child walking with her mother past a field of violets when she felt that God was making a pass at her in the flowers. God is constantly "making a pass" at us in everyday experiences—we simply need to become much more aware of him. People call these experiences *theophanies* (God encounters), and our task as God's sent people is to bring a meaningful interpretation to these experiences and point people to Jesus as the center of the God experience. This is what Keller means by telling people's stories in the light of God's story—the gospel.

### Priests in the Hood (Making Connections between God and People)

Another way to look at this role of seeing "the virtue in the vice" is to conceive of ourselves in terms of one of our deepest identities as disciples, namely, the priesthood of all believers. In *Untamed*, Deb and I suggest that unlocking this is one of the most potent things we can do to allow God to work through all of his people. A priest is essentially someone who mediates the knowledge of God. Our priestly role therefore is to introduce people to Jesus and Jesus to people, and as far as we can, make sure that it is a right understanding of Jesus that we are mediating, and then step out of the way—let Jesus do his thing with people. He knows exactly how to deal with them.

### What Is Good News for This People?

As we have seen, a missionary is essentially a messenger obligated to somehow deliver the message in a way it can be received. This means that we have to be able to speak meaningfully into a culture, but in order to do that, we have to seriously examine a given culture for clues to what God is doing among a people. One of the best ways to start this "listening process" is to go to your tribe. And standing where they stand, and having explored the dynamics of their search, simply ask yourself this question: "What is good news for this people?" What is going to make them throw a party and invite their friends? This is exactly what Matthew did (Matt. 9:9–13). This will mean trying to delve into the existential issues a people or cultural group deals with. It means searching for signs of the quest for meaning and therefore for God. Just like Paul in Athens (Acts 17), it will also mean a study of the religion, art, and literature of the group.

### Follow the Ant Trails

Once we have named the existential issues that our adopted tribe faces, our task will then turn to developing communities (because that's what good mission aims at—a community of Jesus disciples). In the debriefing at the end of the book, we will look at how we might reframe our understanding of church. At this point it might simply mean asking the question, What is church going to look like for this particular tribe of

**Volunteering, according to Mark Van S**

Most urban areas have social service organizations in place. I suggest you volunteer with them instead of starting church programs—at least early on in the life of your church. In the West part of our city, there are over a dozen organizations that will take volunteers. When we started, we tried to do our own English as a Second Language program. It didn't work like we wanted. I'm realizing now that it would have been better to put our energy towards volunteering at existing ESL courses. When we volunteer, we submit to the service organizations—yielding to their agenda instead of forcing our own. In that place, we can begin to make relationships with people. As we meet people and get to know them, we have the opportunity to take that friendship outside of the volunteer organization. As we find out more of their needs, then we may try to serve them as a church.

The basic idea is this: utilize existing structures. Build relationships within the existing systems. Social services provide a great way for you to meet people (both volunteers and those with needs) without having to put a lot of time and energy into planning. You get the benefit of meeting people by simply volunteering. And you will grow in your understanding of the people you want to serve. Plus, you are helping people. And too many churches don't do enough of that.

This, of course, doesn't mean that a church should never start programs. A church may be obligated to do so because there is a profoundly unmet need. Or you may be led to do so; these are simply suggestions to help you think through being incarnational, not hard-and-fast rules. [7]

people? To answer this will require that you look at the social patterning of the group. Follow the ant trails and they will lead you to the "nest." Where do they meet? Why do they meet? What is the cultural dynamic of the group? And once you have done this, try to articulate what an authentic expression of church might look like within that cultural setting. If it's a tribe that meets regularly at the local pub, then it's pretty easy. If it's a group of mountain bikers, it might be a bit more difficult, but you can be sure they meet somewhere. The aim will be to incarnate the gospel in the place by first planting the gospel (Jesus) and then allowing a local and indigenous expression of community to grow out of that encounter.

## Experiencing Seamlessness

One of the important dimensions of incarnational mission is to somehow break the dualistic impasse that seems to exist between various aspects of our worlds. We experience God, church, and the rest of life as being in separate, nonintersecting compartments. We live as if there is an insurmountable distance between the "sacred" and the "secular." But if Jesus is Lord of all of life, there is no such distinction.

The bad scripting downloads through the way we do church: the language and experience of church is generally worlds away from our experience of work, play, politics, etc. In fact they all seem to be so disparate and exist on their own autonomous principles. The world of commerce, for instance, seems to run on its own principles (e.g., radical competition), ones that you would never apply to your personal relationships and family (which requires a fundamental cooperation), or vice versa. Living under the lordship of Jesus requires that we bring all elements into relation with him—we cannot exclude dimensions from God's concern or we create dark zones that invite the idols to enslave us. The way I illustrate this in *The Forgotten Ways* is as follows:[8]

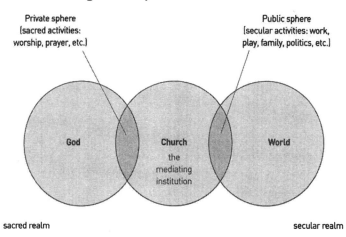

Private sphere
(sacred activities: worship, prayer, etc.)

Public sphere
(secular activities: work, play, family, politics, etc.)

God

Church
the mediating institution

World

sacred realm

secular realm

## The Dualistic Christendom Mode

Here our "worlds" never seem to meet but rather are experienced as pulling in opposite directions. We divide our worlds into the sacred (on the left) and the secular (on the right), and they are experienced as worlds apart. Incarnational approaches try to see the kingdom in all elements of life and seek to bring the dimensions closer. We take the church with us into the world, because in the deepest possible way, we *are* the church.

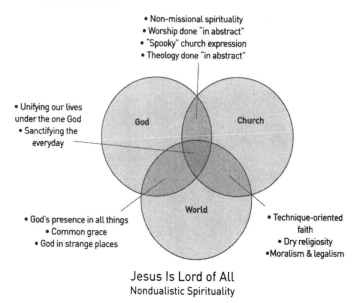

Jesus Is Lord of All
Nondualistic Spirituality

Moving deeper therefore means bringing the disparate elements of life together in a way that creates a more seamless experience of the Christian life. We allow our various worlds to collide. We try to be the same person in at least three places—church, home, and work—but an integrated, incarnational spirituality also means that the gospel seeps into the nooks and crannies of our lives.

So to sum up, we first move out and then move in. Or as incarnational missionary Mark Van Steenwyk wisely advises,

Once you move into the area (or if you already live in the area), spend time just observing. Don't get frenetic. Don't start doing things until you understand the ethos of the neighborhood. Let the spirit of the place make its impression. Fall in love with the little things. Get to know the people. If you start "doing your thing" before you are familiar with the place, then you're forcing things too much. Ministry should fit with how God is already working in a place. If you start pushing your agenda before you start making friends with the neighbors and finding out about their lives, then you're a salesman, not a minister of reconciliation. And throughout it all, pray. Pray for spiritual eyesight. It is the Spirit's job to reveal Christ . . . not just to "them" but also to "you." Pray that you can see Christ's fingerprints in your neighborhood. Pray to see the face of Christ in the face of those who live around you. Pray for the Spirit to show you what is wrong in your area, and also what is right. Seek to understand.[9]

## Move Alongside (Urbs and Relationships)

### SUBurb: A Theology of Geography/Place

The reality is, to become a missional Christian, we begin by simply paying attention to the neighborhood and the relationships in various aspects of our life. But if the tribe you are seeking to touch with the love of Jesus lives in another part of town (or in the case of a missionary, overseas), you will need to seriously consider relocating. It is interesting that our Lord is called Jesus of Nazareth. So it's clear that Jesus got into Nazareth, but I have often found myself wondering how much of Nazareth got into Jesus. The truth is that in the incarnation, Jesus took up residence in Nazareth, in ancient Judea, among a distinct people, and became one of them.

We used the idea of being the priest in the hood above. Well, just like a local gang, we should have a "turf." When seeking to touch a people, an urban tribe, it is no good simply visiting their area and then traveling over half an hour to get home.

You should live where you want to serve. You should be able to bump into the tribe in the local shops and supermarket. This allows for what I call three practices of incarnational engagement: proximity, frequency, and spontaneity.[10]

### Ground Control to Major Tom: Making Contact

In Western settings, we should simply assume that all communication of the gospel is cross-cultural. If you do this, at least you won't make the mistake of assuming the same worldview and beliefs as the people you are trying to reach. Train yourself to be inclusive and invitational in posture. And while the missional posture requires a go-to-them approach, it will also be an invitation to relationship. So find ways to invite people into your life: to a BBQ, to a party, or whatever. And remember to talk as if nonbelieving people are present—learn to drop the insider/church lingo. Tim Keller says that if you speak and converse *as if* your whole neighborhood is present (not just scattered Christians), eventually more and more of your neighborhood will find their way into your life and community and feel a part of it.[11]

### Beyond Functional Friendships

In *Untamed*[12] Deb and I suggest that for the large part, we have generally misinterpreted the Great Commission (Matt. 28:18–20) as an *evangelistic* text, whereas in fact it is a *discipling* text. It is not about simply sharing the Good News with people through abstract concepts about Jesus and calling for a response—this is at best only part of the deal, at worst a shoddy witness and mere salesmanship. Friendships should be part of the equation. We are called to disciple the nations, which means we are committed to a long-term relationship with them that must surely include meaningful friendships, genuine involvement, and compassionate concern for a person's best good. Christians should know how to be the best friends a person can have, because friendship (in the truest sense of discipleship) lies at the heart of the biblical commission. Think of the Great Commission in this way: as pre-conversion discipleship AND post-conversion discipleship, but it is discipleship all along the way.

### The Art of Conversation(s)

In many ways this recipe is part cultural savvy, part organic friendship, and part hospitality, but in our experience Christians are not necessarily good at conversation. We tend toward functionality in our relationships, we lack cultural breadth, and we are too quick to want to get to the Bible and spirituality. In short, we should strive to be more culturally interesting. For men, sports features quite strongly in conversation, and for women, family and relational issues. Whatever the content, genuinely artful conversation uses all of these in a dialogue that is authentically conversational—subtle, spiritual, and culturally tuned to the issues of the day—to really engage people at the level of their lives and story. Remember, pop culture is where people live! Be aware of what's going on at that level. And stop being overly "spiritual," using insider, religious language, to talk about God—it mostly alienates people. Rather, bring a God interpretation to ordinary life without forcing conversations to the four spiritual laws.

Conversation invites friendship, provokes intrigue, promotes mutual quest, weaves story with opinion, extends a listening ear, and offers something of the self in the equation. At best it is done around tables or in places of social engagement. And make no mistake; it is a powerful way of missionally engaging people. In *Untamed* we suggest that if every Christian family in the world simply offered good conversational hospitality around a table once a week to neighbors, we would eat our way into the kingdom of God.

### Sneezing the Gospel

In *The Forgotten Ways* I suggest that all good ideas spread like viruses and that the gospel, insofar that it is an idea (of course it is more than that), is no exception. In other words, we "sneeze" the gospel into various social settings as we let it travel along relational lines.[13]

This phenomenon of viral movements is demonstrated in the power of social networking so prevalent in our day. To be missional disciples, we need to learn how to use the power of ideas and relationships and bring these together. To do this we need rich relationships, or in terms of people movements, lots of "social surface" to be big influencers in people's lives. The greater the social surface, the higher the likelihood of influence/spread, and therefore missional impact. It is important to remember this because the gospel always travels along and within the relational fabric of a given culture.[14] Missional Christianity needs to get relationally savvy, and it should come naturally because we are called to love and discipleship.[15]

### Matthew's Party

In Luke 10 Jesus sends the seventy out with some very sage missional advice. Among other things he tells them not to start groups in their own houses but to "go" to people's houses and start things up there. The reason? Well, it is their turf, and because of that they are most likely to invite their friends to a social gathering that they host. If it was at your place, they might come but are unlikely to invite their friends.

The principle here is that we should be aware of social dynamics and the role of gatekeepers. It's part of relational savvy-ness mentioned above. Missionaries have long understood that identifying the person who holds "the keys" to entry to the tribe plays a strategic role in reaching that tribe. Without being manipulative about it, we would be wise to focus on such people. If they open up to us (and God), then they in turn will win their own social circle over.

Matthew the tax collector is a case in point (Matt. 9:9–13). Mathew becomes a disciple and holds a party where he invites all his friends. Zacchaeus does the same thing (Luke 19:2–10). They don't have to go to church or to a house church to meet Jesus. He comes to them. And this is not equivalent to using people, because we choose to love them authentically in their own world; it just means being strategic with our time and influence.

So to develop missionality right here, right now, we move *out*, move *in*, move *alongside*, and as we shall now see, sometimes move *from*.

## Move From (Subvert)

Contrary to a narrow fundamentalist understanding of things, the gospel does not challenge or undermine *everything* in any given culture. There are many good things that are entirely consistent with a biblical understanding of society and life. For example, non-Christians who value speaking the truth, doing good to others, and living outwardly moral lives. Theologians have always called this *common grace*. These include aspects of culture that can be affirmed and deepened by coming into contact with the gospel of Jesus Christ. However, there will be things in any culture (including our own) that jar up against what Jesus teaches—aspects that are ungodly and dehumanizing. It is the missional Christian's duty to be very discerning here, because failure to recognize the deficiencies in our own culture means that we will simply impose our culture (and sometimes not the gospel) on a people group or tribe. But when it comes to being missional right here and right now, sometimes we are simply going to have to issue a direct challenge, or in the language of this heading "move from," in order to bring Good News into the tribe.

## Questioning and the Quest

The truth is that we don't always have to take issues head-on. Sometimes our role is to be undercover subversives. Yes, there are times when we need to be overt and verbal and confrontational, but perhaps not all that often. There is another deeply biblical way of going about bringing profound change in a society. Jesus talked about the kingdom of God as being like yeast that leavens a whole lump without our direct influence. He talked about it being like a field where the farmer plants and waters, and it grows all by itself. In other words, the kingdom works covertly to undermine the way things are now and to initiate God's rule in its place. Scholars call this aspect of Jesus' teaching of the kingdom "the now and the not-yet." Some people see it and respond. Others cannot see it at all. One day God will concentrate it all to a point and close the deal once and for all. But we can be sure the kingdom is here right now . . . active in the entire world, but especially through his people.

Many times in pastoral work, when we have brought someone to the Lord who was sleeping with his/her partner, we didn't throw the rule book at them. Rather, we would introduce them to Jesus and trust that the couple would come to the right conclusions themselves. We would plant good seeds, water them, and voilà, the Holy Spirit would do his work.

The parables are classical tools of subversion. In *The Shaping of Things to Come*, Michael and I probe why Jesus never seems to answer a question directly.[16] Sometimes he answers with a counterquestion. But most often he uses parables. Now a parable is not some cute little illustration to make things clear. In fact, Jesus says that they are quite the opposite—they are puzzles that can really confuse the hearers (Matt. 13:1–23). They are not clear-cut, three-point sermons with good illustrations to boot. They are designed to provoke a search—a quest—in which the hearer is invited to fill in the blanks for themselves. And clearly they are subversive, because some get it and some miss the point. Some like what they hear and others hate it.

## Lifestyle

The most consistent way to challenge the destructive forces in popular culture is to live contrary to them—to actually *be* the change we want to see. In a world obsessed with consumerism, we choose to live more simply. In a world obsessed with social status and image, we choose to associate with poor, "invisible," and uncool people and invite them into our lives. In a world obsessed with money, we choose to be very generous. In other words, without withdrawing ourselves from our tribe, we have to model what a Jesus alternative looks like to our tribe. They must see the gospel embodied in us, for in the end, the medium *is* the message.[17]

In relation to lifestyle, Tim Keller suggests that

> in a missional church, . . . Christian community must go beyond that to embody a "counter-culture," showing the world how radically different a Christian society is with regard to sex, money, and power. . . .
>
> • In money. We promote a radically generous commitment of time, money, relationships, and living space to social justice and the needs of the poor, the immigrant, the economically and physically weak.
>
> • In power. We are committed to power sharing and relationship-building between genders, races, and classes that are alienated outside of the Body of Christ.
>
> In general, a church must be more deeply and practically committed to deeds of compassion and social justice than traditional liberal churches and more deeply and practically committed to evangelism and conversion than traditional fundamentalist churches. This kind of church is profoundly "counter-intuitive" to American observers. It breaks their

ability to categorize (and dismiss) it as liberal or conservative. Only this kind of church has any chance in the non-Christian West.[18]

### Community

One of the most profound ways to embody countercultural dissents against the evil propensities in our cultures is to embody the gospel in a community of Jesus' people. It has been said that the real task of Christians is to be the church rather than to transform the world. In other words, the church doesn't *have* a social strategy, the church *is* the social strategy. Here we get to show the world a certain type of life the world can never achieve through social coercion or governmental action.

When the church gets its act together, it is the most potent force for the transformation of the world.[19] When we try putting into effect a Christian political agenda/party, we inevitably mess it up—if the European Christendom experience taught us anything, it taught us this. Most Christian political parties end up being domineering, angry, religious bullies operating through coercive power—hardly consistent with Jesus' approach to changing the world. In fact, we end up looking more like Jesus' opponents—the scribes, Sadducees, Zealots, and Pharisees.

This communal aspect is also why missionality is not the work of a lone ranger that is so much part of the American individualistic mythology. The kind of change God requires of the world can only be achieved through communal action. It's the trick that God has played on our individualism. We can do truly great things only when we find each other and do it together. This is the realm of *missional church*, and we are all part of it. Besides, a community that embodies the life and teachings of Jesus is the kind of community that is itself deeply attractive to a lonely and lost world. The best thing we can do is simply become ourselves and live it out as authentically as we can.

## Sexuality

We live in a world obsessed by sex. Clearly this presents a challenge to our view of the world. Quite honestly I am not sure that historically we have done a good job of representing God on this one. We have largely been experienced as life-suppressing moralists and/or dangerous bigots. The reality is that our Lord Jesus actually dealt very mercifully with "sexual sinners" (e.g., Luke 7:36–50; John 8:1–11) and extremely harshly with self-righteous moralists (e.g., Matt. 23). The church should become more like Jesus on this one.

Speaking from within his experience of New York's urban context, Tim Keller suggests that we should avoid both the secular society's idolization of sex and traditional society's fear of sex. "We must also exhibit love rather than hostility or fear toward those whose sexual life-patterns are different."[20] Too right! The issue is that we must demonstrate an alternative vision of sexuality, but we must do so without being moralistic. People are watching us on this.

<<< >>>

OK, enough. Well, at least enough to make a good start of being a darn good missional disciple in any context we might find ourselves in. We have explored four aspects of what it means to be a movement: move *out*, move *in*, move *alongside*, move *from*.

Needless to say, all this is well within your power and means. Jesus designed you for influence, change, and impact, right here, right now. And in your healing and salvation lies the healing and salvation of others around you and through you. You simply have to live it in ways that are meaningful and accessible to all. Our lives, for his glory, and for his kingdom—this is our true worship.

SECTION ONE

# PUTTING OUR HEARTS INTO IT

*(MISSIONAL PARADIGM)*

>>> **1**

# PUTTING THE EXTRA
# IN THE ORDINARY

*Viewing Daily Life with a Missionary's Eye*

> Here's the church
> Here's the steeple
> Open the doors
> And there's all the people

In the words of Dana Carvey's Church Lady, "Isn't that special?" Well, no, it's really not. Call me a theological prude, but I think it is pretty awful. But just about anyone who grew up in church will recognize this little children's rhyme. And at first glance it seems cute and innocent enough, but it reinforces, at an early and impressionable age, the skewed viewpoint that church is a *building* and it is the primary place where the people of God are to be found.

In our day, we are seeing this edifice-complex idea of the church begin to erode. More and more, we are seeing instances of pastors and church leaders chipping away at the wrong-headed idea of church as an event or location. Leaders are helping their congregations to understand and confidently embrace the call to ministry that God has placed on their lives. Christians everywhere are beginning to see their callings are just as relevant, substantial, and certifiable as any "professional" ministry position.

## Me, a Missionary?

Have you ever heard the Scott Wesley Brown song, "Please Don't Send Me to Africa"? Like any good comedic piece, it's a fun parody because it echoes a lot of truth about our ideas—in this case, of the call of a missionary life. As the song goes, we give God a nice, long list of how we've served him—albeit quite comfortably in our middle-class suburbia—and then make deals with him so he won't send us to "the bush."

The first time I heard the song, I thought, "This guy must have grown up in *my* church." My idea of a missionary was fueled by summer visits to our church from missionary families. This was the time of year that the missionary families were "on furlough," which even as a youngster sounded to me like a temporary break from army duty. They would give Kodak slide presentations of their work when they visited the churches that funded them. I would count ceiling tiles as the projector clicked off one picture after another. I wanted to hear stories about tiger attacks and dodging poison darts. As a youngster all the presentations seemed to depict a white family living amidst tribal people in Papua New Guinea or Nairobi, or working with little Australian Aborigines. I wondered what these poor Americans had done to make God mad enough to send them to such places. To me, missionary life meant no Pop-Tarts for breakfast, no Fleetwood Mac eight tracks, and no Dallas Cowboys on Sunday afternoons.

In the fellowship hall after one of these presentations, I told one of my friends, "I'll never be a missionary. I'm gonna ask God to never send me to one of those places." One of the old ladies in our church overheard what I said, shook a nine-inch finger in my face and said, "You better not say that, young man, because if you do, that's exactly where God will send you!" I looked at her bug-eyed, and gulped. I thought to myself, "I've done it now. Ten years old, and my life is done for." That pretty much summed up my concept of missions. As I grew older, I admired the missionaries and felt an allegiance to support them financially, but I did not see myself in any way, shape, or form as a missionary. In my mind, missions were something that happened across borders, in faraway places. To be a missionary you had to move to a foreign land. I certainly didn't feel called to move to any particular faraway place or people, so I knew for sure I wasn't called to be a missionary. From that point on, when I heard the word "missionary," there was an immediate mental disconnect between that word and me.

## Missionary in the Mirror

Through many years and conversations with other Christians and church leaders, I came to realize that my concept of a missionary was pretty much the norm. Most of us have viewed missions as something that happens *over there*. "We have tended to see mission as something we do in 'heathen nations' and not on home base. We evangelize *here* and do *mission* there. This has rightly been called the 'geographic myth.'"[1]

The reality is that *all* Christians are not only called to be missionaries but have already been *sent* to the people they are called to reach. Christians who earn a living as teachers, accountants, store clerks, mechanics, plumbers, doctors, whatever—you are a missionary! This is not to cheapen the definition of a missionary. I'm not suggesting that there

## JUST SAYIN'...

Unless the church recovers its role as a subversive, missionary movement, by re-instilling the vision within the people of God that we are all indeed God's missionary people, the present and subsequent generations will find very little interest in our static agendas.
A complete paradigm shift is essential for the Western church to avoid becoming an anemic shell of its former self. If we have any realistic hope of recovering the Christian witness in the West, the church must abandon the diluted role and shortsighted vision as a static institution and dive headlong into its original calling as a missionary movement.

—*Alan Hirsch*

are not certain members of the body of Christ who *are* called by the Lord to serve in locations that necessitate relocating and learning native languages and customs. There absolutely are. Many of these Christians are my personal heroes.

What has been missing, however, is a broader understanding and imagination of *who* is both qualified and conscribed to missions. Every Christian needs to view his or her immediate world with the same perspective as a missionary in a foreign land. The best hope for the spread of kingdom outposts is for our churches to consist of *individuals* who view themselves as missionaries. A missionary sees the immediate world with different eyes than does the native citizen. If you have ever participated in a short-term mission trip, you have a taste of what this feels like. On trips to Afghanistan, Mexico, or throughout Southeast Asia, each day I would wake up with eyes and heart wide open to see and hear what God might say or what opportunity there might be to touch a life. I packed light and spent with thrift to avoid being bogged down and to be able to help others when I came across a need. My prayers were intense and the desire for wisdom and faith was high. Most days were met with eager expectation and deep reliance upon the Holy Spirit for guidance.

Our churches can have wonderfully written missional vision statements and well-conceived plans and programs. But if individual members are not committed to living their lives as kingdom-minded missionaries in their daily life stations, then the corporate efforts of the church as a whole will never sniff the air of their true kingdom potential.

It is impossible to be a missional *church* if we fail to be missional *people*. Otherwise, missionality is reduced to sponsored programs that centralize the life of the body of Christ, institutionalizing and containing it in church systems and programs that view mission as something that happens "over there" or at special events.

One evening I was driving home from a planning meeting at our church offices where we had just scheduled a servant-kindness project. By that point we had done dozens of such projects, but this time something hit me as strange and unnatural about this. It just felt somewhat contrived and artificial. I had to admit to myself that I was about 50 percent friendlier to strangers during these special events than I was the rest of the time. I realized I was clocking in for the "good works" hour and clocking out when it was over. I thought to myself, "Rather than training our people to *do* kindness and generosity for a couple of hours, why don't we train them to *be* kind and generous . . . all the time?"

Serving events can be great primers and training camps for developing and sharpening the missional heart, but these alone will fail to develop full-fledged missional movements in our fellowships. Churches that organize themselves in a missional orientation view *mission* as something that happens *right here and right now* through all members of the church all of the time. There is a huge difference in a church organizing itself around church services, sermons, and great worship events over and against a church that takes up its position and mandate as a missionary for its culture. This has nothing to do with church size—mega, medium, or small church.

65

**JUST SAYIN'...**

A working definition of *missional church* is a community of God's people that defines itself by, and organizes its life around, its real purpose of being an agent of God's mission to the world. In other words, the church's true and authentic "organizing principle" is mission. When the church is on mission, it is the true church. The church itself is not only the result of God's mission but is obligated and destined to extend it by whatever means possible. The mission of God flows directly through every believer and every community of faith that adheres to Jesus. To obstruct this is to block God's purposes in and through his people.

*—Alan Hirsch*

My good friend Bob Roberts and his wife saw their church (Northwood Church in Keller, TX) totally transformed several years ago. In the midst of lamenting that their desire to work in a foreign mission field was not going to happen, he had a life-altering thought: "What if the *church* viewed itself as a missionary?" In other words, rather than just looking for people who could be sent to a foreign field, what might happen if a local church began to view *itself* as a missionary in its local setting? Bob began to ask, "What would be the effect if a local church began to train its members to live with the same fervor, goals, and mindset of a missionary who had been sent to a foreign field? Plus, what would happen if that same church also went to foreign fields as well and committed itself to entire people groups, pouring its combined talents and resources into transformative synergy?"

The results have been nothing short of phenomenal—significant transformation has been made in several foreign nations, plus "average" church members literally *live* for mission, realigning priorities, schedules, and financial planning from a missional commitment. It is not uncommon to hear of entire families giving up the yearly vacation to Disney World or Yosemite to go serve in Vietnam or Mexico. These same families have also made deep connections with Vietnamese and Mexican population pockets in their own community. They give themselves to learn the culture and traditions of these people groups, mixing their lives with them. They are a glocal (global + local) missional people.

Does this mean the church Bob serves does not have a well-organized Sunday morning experience? Not at all. Northwood is a megachurch, with all the accompanying bells and whistles, and energetic, uplifting church services. But the lifeblood of Northwood Church flows from its missionary character. If you aren't keen on mission or just want feel-good messages, you will not stay there long. Bob and his team will drive you nuts to get on mission.

Mission as organizing principle means that mission goes way beyond being some sort of optional activity or program for our churches. It actually is the organizing axis of the church. The life of the church revolves around it. This is not to say that we don't do corporate worship, develop community, and make disciples, but that these are catalyzed by and organized around the mission function. Only in this way can we be truly missional. Merely adding serving events or special outreach days to our church schedules will not develop missional *people* nor make a missional church.

## No Average Joes

It is essential for the average Joe and Jill Churchperson to cease viewing themselves as *average*. Leaders must also stop viewing them this way as well. There is nothing remotely average about a human being who has been born again with the very resurrection life that caused Jesus to rise from the dead (see Eph. 2:3–10), to have the indwelling Holy Spirit as guide, to possess the mind of Christ for needed wisdom, and then to be commissioned by Jesus himself to go into the world with his redemptive agenda.

It is an affront to the person and work of Jesus for any Christian to view himself or herself as a mere church member. I don't say this in order to patronize and pump up the injured or unhealthy self-esteem of some readers. The facts and outcome of redemption through the blood of Jesus is that the very life and power of Jesus is in *every* Christian. We are all equipped to minister right here and right now, regardless of what that "here and now" is. Consider the words of the apostle Paul: "And God is able to make all grace abound to you, so that in all things at all times, having all that you need, you will abound in every good work" (2 Cor. 9:8).

God is not limited. To the contrary, he is *able* to make his grace fill up anything lacking in us. Paul says that not only will we have all that we need, we will *abound* in every good work. For a group of Christians, regardless of size, to take on this understanding and perspective is a powerful thing to consider. The potential for real community transformation is enormous when "average" Christians pick up the mantle of servanthood. It happens as we take upon ourselves the responsibility to see that those we encounter on a day-to-day basis are blessed, and we take seriously our own roles as ambassadors of the kingdom of God.

This means we don't place the responsibility for outreach events on the church staff. When we realize this and act on it, the number of those involved in "ministry" increases exponentially. All the while Christian living moves from living safe and secure (even boring) lives to a life of solid purpose and engagement in the adventure of advancing the kingdom agenda of the gospel of Jesus Christ. It really changes everything about our lives and pursuits.

Recently a suburban mother of three decided to take seriously Jesus' words about inviting strangers and outcasts to your table when you throw a party. As Christmas Day 2008 approached, Colleen Norton chose to reach out to others by placing a simple ad on Craigslist that read:

### Free Christmas Dinner with New Friends

Are you hitting hard times or lonely and want to have a nice Christmas dinner? Please come and celebrate with my loving family. Please email for my address. Thank you and God Bless.

Thirty people responded to Colleen's ad, many wanting to donate food, and six (previously) strangers, including a mother and her two sons, joined Colleen's family for Christmas dinner. One lady said she responded to the ad because her husband was in the hospital recovering from a stroke and she had no one to spend Christmas day with. Colleen said she hopes to teach her three daughters the importance of helping others and that Christmas is about reaching out to others. "I like to believe that my girls learn that they're really blessed in life," she said. "If we were hitting hard times, we would hope that someone would be there for us."

Colleen simply considered her resources, made herself available, and stepped out of the ordinary into the extraordinary. She ignored her limitations and considered what she *could* do over and above what she could not do.

This is a shift from *Jesus fan* to full-time player on Team Jesus. It happens as ministry moves out of the church box and into the landscape of everyday life. It is misguided to say, "I'm in *full-time* ministry," implying that Christians who don't get their paycheck from a church or Christian organization are only in *part-time* ministry. We might as well be saying, "I'm a pro; you're just an amateur." The Jesus edict couldn't be clearer. He calls all Christians as full-time ambassadors of his kingdom, regardless of vocation or the way they earn their living. As he prays to the Father, shortly before betrayal and crucifixion, Jesus underscores the missional commissioning of his disciples: "In the same way that you gave me a mission in the world, I give them a mission in the world" (John 17:18 Message).

## JUST SAYIN'...

If we will just allow our imaginations to be handed over to God, missional creativity and expression will explode in ways we would never have imagined before. In *Untamed*, Debra and I bring up the issue of creativity and its essence as being from the Creator, God himself: "A sanctified imagination is a powerful tool because the fundamental job of the imagination in life is to produce, out of the society we have to live in, a vision of the society we want to live in."[2]

—*Alan Hirsch*

Jesus says, "My disciples are sent on mission, just like I was sent on mission." To be *like* Jesus means we not only embrace his character and message, but we embrace his mission as well.

## Want Joy? I'll Give You Joy

This calling and sending action not only forms our identity as the people of God, but it is tied directly to our purpose for life. Joy and contentment are direct by-products of *being* and *doing* who and what we are called by God to both be and do. When most of our energy and resources are spent on things other than our God-given purpose and call, we become drained and hollow. We become like caged birds, with clipped wings. Birds were not created to be in cages but were meant to take flight. But as we open our eyes to the hurts and needs around us, and we make our time and resources available to God and others, our hearts grow and our lives are filled with *true* joy. Sending us on mission is one of the greatest gifts God could give us. Something almost mystical takes place when we reach out to others to help and heal them. Jesus mentions the joy factor in the John 17 prayer, just a few sentences before the verse we just read: "I'm saying these things in the world's hearing so my people can experience my joy completed in them" (John 17:13 Message).

Many psychologists conclude that the majority of emotional and spiritual disorders are not the result of damaged psyches but of disconnected people. The premise is that when two people connect on a significant level, something is poured out of one into the other that has the power to heal the soul of its deepest wounds and create restoration. We are wired by God to both need and be needed by others. Over two decades of pastoring has taught me that the people who refuse to help others are the ones who remain most needy themselves. On the other hand, some of the most joyful people I've known have been the most selfless, although their own circumstances were hard or less than ideal.

Perhaps the greatest factor that hinders the Western church from missional engagement is that most Christians here do not identify themselves as fully empowered agents of the kingdom of God. Most Christians have allowed their identity and life purpose to be shaped by the surrounding culture. This leaves God's agenda—the agenda of his kingdom—languishing. The mission of God gets people's leftovers. The remaining scraps from earthly pursuits are tossed God's way. Intercultural ministry specialist Dan Devadatta speaks to this critical issue:

> Consider Abraham, the father of our faith, who went to the foreign land of the Hittites and said, "I am a stranger and sojourner among you" (Genesis 23:4). Or consider the Psalmist, who made confession of the fleeting nature of human life when he wrote, "I am your passing guest, a sojourner, like all my fathers" (Psalm 39:12). Or consider in our own time the familiar song we sing, "This world is not my home, I am just passing through." The picture of the normal Christian life and community is that we have been chosen to live our days as strangers whose citizenship is not on earth. Our citizenship, instead, is in a city that God himself is making.[3]

Our hunch is that most all Christians have genuinely deep and sincere desires to live their lives with meaningful purpose that goes beyond selfish gain or temporal earthly pursuits; they just don't know how or what to do. The phenomenal success of Rick Warren's book, *The Purpose-Driven Life,* bears testimony to this. Furthermore, most church leaders are at a loss to define on both a conceptual and practical basis the true purpose of the saints in their churches.

## The Times, They Are A-Changinged

For the North American church, a major game-changer has come about over the last half century. As the final decades of the twentieth century progressed, the door began to close on the church as having a privileged position in contemporary society. There are many signs of this. In the Midwest and South (in the US) prior to the late 1980s, you would never see children's sports leagues schedule games on Sundays. I know by experience, growing up in Texas in the 1970s, Little League baseball games and even practices would never take place on Wednesdays because of the influence of evangelicals and church services on Wednesday nights. Youth event organizers and public school officials would not think of scheduling events late in the day on Wednesday in deference to local churches.

Statistically speaking, church attendance began to slide at an enormous rate, and Sunday, for instance, lost its place as a sacred day in North America. Blue laws (statutes that prohibited many products from being sold on Sundays) left the books, and department stores and other businesses started opening their doors on Sundays. This signaled the final chapter on the age of Constantinian[4] Christendom, where the church stood front and center, influence-wise, in communities. Author and editor Rodney Clapp says:

> Christians feel useless because the church feels useless. And the church feels useless because it keeps on trying to perform Constantinian duties in a world that is no longer Constantinian. So the grace is this: Christians feel useless because they are no longer useful for the wrong thing, namely serving as chaplains in a sponsorial religion.[5]

I remember my (public) elementary school days in the early 1970s. Each morning began with the principal praying over an intercom as each classroom stood at attention, with hand over heart. The Ten Commandments hung in each classroom and there was no concern of lawsuits or Supreme Court intervention.

These were times when Christianity was supported and reinforced through many entities such as education and political and civic organizations. Many Christians lament the passing of these days, believing that the church is to occupy a dominative position and create a Christian nation-state. The present situation has left many in the church confused and frustrated. It is a struggle for identity, with some churches and Christians fighting to regain the lost position as chaplain for society.

The reality of our situation is that Christendom has been in decline for the last 250 years. This is what the term *post-Christendom* means. Society, at least in its overtly, non-Christian manifestation, is "over" Christendom. The problem for many Christians and church leaders is that we have not come to grips with this fact. We fight for prayers and the Ten Com-

## JUST SAYIN'...

If time travel existed and we were transported to the first three centuries of the church, most of us would not recognize it as church because it has none of the outward forms and little of the traditional characteristics of what we normally call "church." We inhabit a much more institutional "idea of church" than that of our early forebears. And not all of it is bad. But what has been highly damaging is the present-day way of being and doing church that arose from it becoming the official, state-sponsored religion. As a result, mission was trivialized to being a marginal, undeveloped, unloved subset of the church rather than being its organizing principle. This has distorted our sense of identity and our purpose as God's people from being a dynamic, transformative movement to being a static, religious institution.

—*Alan Hirsch*

mandments to stay posted in courtrooms because we think Christianity is the dominant civil religion and ought to be so. In other words, we still think of the church and its mission in terms of Christendom, while in reality we are in a post-Christendom context. The Western church still operates for the most part in a Christendom mode. People who fail to come to grips with the end of Christendom remind me of the legends of Japanese soldiers holed up for several years in tunnels on the island of Iowa Jima. They refused to believe that World War II was over. They eventually had to come out and learn to live in a postwar culture.

Alan and I believe that the end of Christendom is not bad news. To the contrary, it is forcing us all to dig deeply to reimagine and reconsider the purpose and position of the church. It is causing massive numbers of Christians to awaken to something dormant in their lives. They are coming to realize that their calling is every bit as genuine and relevant as seminary-trained professional clergy.

No longer should any of us expect to be able to set up a church in the midst of a community and have the "build it and they will come" *Field of Dreams* phenomena take place. Rather, we must develop pockets of believers embedded throughout the community that draw life from the well of redemption and see their own lives as available way stations for thirsty travelers.

### Where Are *You* From, Partner?

One evening Alan and I were eating at one of those Texas-themed steak houses, and the servers were singing a chorus that refrained with the phrase "Yee haw!" With a smirk, Alan said to me, "You Texans . . . *Yee haw!*" I said, "You Aussies . . . *By crickey!*" This created a spirited argument where I felt obliged to defend the Texan motherland. I argued that this saying is nothing more than an old-time B-Western movie phrase that has nothing to do with modern-day Texans. "Texans don't go around saying, 'Yee haw,'" I told him. I also made the point that most Texans don't ride horses, wear cowboy hats, or have spurs that jingle, jangle, jingle. Alan tried to convince me that "by crickey" was not a phrase used by the typical Aussie, nor do most of them run around with horse whips tied to their belts and hunting knifes slid into their boots. The fact is, we all expect people from certain places to speak, dress, and pursue a certain set of styles, ideas, and agendas. We expect people loyal to their homeland to buy into and live by the values and goals of their citizenry.

This is especially true of ambassadors: they are diplomatic representatives of their home country who are commissioned to represent the interests and goals of their homeland. And this is very much the mantle that all Christians are commissioned to pick up. The apostle Paul emphasized the issue of a heavenly citizenship throughout his letters to the churches—a theme that Paul drew directly from Jesus: "Their mind is on earthly things. But our citizen-

## JUST SAYIN'. . .

Speaking of the early Christian communities in the Roman Empire, the author of *The Epistle of Mathetes to Diognetus* wrote in the second century,

They dwell in their own countries, but simply as sojourners. As citizens, they share in all things with others, and yet endure all things as if foreigners. Every foreign land is to them as their native country, and every land of their birth as a land of strangers. They marry, as do all [others]; they beget children; but they do not destroy their offspring. They have a common table, but not a common bed. They are in the flesh, but they do not live after the flesh. They pass their days on earth, but they are citizens of heaven. They obey the prescribed laws, and at the same time surpass the laws by their lives. They love all men, and are persecuted by all. They are unknown and condemned; they are put to death, and restored to life. They are poor, yet make many rich; they are in lack of all things, and yet abound in all; they are dishonoured, and yet in their very dishonour are glorified.[6]

*— Alan Hirsch*

75

ship is in heaven. And we eagerly await a Savior from there, the Lord Jesus Christ" (Phil. 3:19–20).

Most scholars agree that there is no significant distinction between the New Testament phrases *kingdom of God* and *kingdom of heaven*. It should catch our attention that these phrases are used over eighty times in the Gospels regarding Jesus' message and agenda, while the word *church* is used a mere three times in all of the Gospels. It is also intriguing that the word *disciple* is used over 260 times in the Gospels alone. I point this out because of the undeniable fact that the vast majority of Christians and Christian leaders emphasize *church* but give scant attention to the kingdom of God and disciple making. We are pretty much obsessed with church but only *favorable* toward the kingdom of God.

The word *kingdom*, as used in the New Testament, is the Greek word *basileia*. It connotes the idea of both the manifestation of and the coming reign of God's rule. It entails all that can come about when and where God is ruling. The kingdom of God is the ethic and creed from which Jesus drew and lived out his life. It set the beat for his rhythm of living. As Jesus went about his public ministry, he announced the coming kingdom and gave foretastes of what the full reign of God would eventually entail. He issued an invitation for people to come into the kingdom and to learn a new approach to life in light of the kingdom agenda and heavenly purposes. Dallas Willard speaks to this:

> From the very beginning of his work, those who relied on him had, at his touch, entered the rule, or governance, of God and were receiving its gracious sufficiency. Jesus was not just acting for God but also with God—a little like the way, in a crude metaphor, I act with my power steering, or it with me, when I turn the wheel of my car. And this "governance" is projected onward through those who receive him. When we receive God's gift of life by relying on Christ, we find that God comes to act with us as we rely on him in our actions. That explains why Jesus said that the least in the kingdom

of the heavens are greater than John the Baptist—not, of course, greater in themselves, but as a greater power works along with them. The "greater" is not inherent, a matter of our own substance, but relational. So, C. S. Lewis writes, our faith is not a matter of our hearing what Christ said long ago and "trying to carry it out." Rather, "The real Son of God is at your side. He is beginning to turn you into the same kind of thing as Himself. He is beginning, so to speak, to 'inject' His kind of life and thought, His Zoe [life], into you; beginning to turn the tin soldier into a live man. The part of you that does not like it is the part that is still tin."[7]

### Have You Given Your Life to the Lord?

Living from and toward the advancing kingdom of God means we need to continually audit our lives in light of the priorities and agenda of Jesus himself. Such an approach sets us at odds with many of the pursuits, goals, and pressures of contemporary society. Most Christians are willing to give their *afterlife* to Jesus but want to keep their earthly life for themselves. "Sure, Lord, you can have me when I'm dead, but I want to hold on to the reins of this earthly gig." There is a commonly spoken phrase used by evangelicals regarding someone who has recently turned to the Lord, and I do not want to be overly critical here, but when I hear someone say, "Five people gave their lives to the Lord in our meeting last night," I bristle. I want to ask, "How do you know they gave their lives to the Lord?" You can't know that until some degree of time goes by. As Benjamin Franklin said, "Time is the stuff life is made of." We must watch a person's life to know whether or not they have really surrendered it to the Lord.

When Jesus announced the arrival of the kingdom of God, he said, "*Repent*, for the kingdom of God is at hand." Notice, he did not say, "Adjust." To repent entails a complete turnaround. It means that our entire life is aimed in a new direction, with new goals and pursuits. If I am driving west on

## JUST SAYIN'...

We need to be aware that within middle-class culture there is much that is contrary to authentic gospel values. And this is not a negative statement about middle-class people per se—I myself am from a very middle-class family—but rather to recognize that much that goes by the name is simply a culture preoccupied with safety and security developed mostly in pursuit of what seems to be best for our children. And this is understandable as long as it does not become obsessive. But when these impulses of middle-class culture fuse with consumerism, as they most often do, we can add the obsession with comfort and convenience to the list. And this is not a good mix—at least as far as the gospel, discipleship, and missional church are concerned.

—*Alan Hirsch*

a highway and receive a phone call that instructs me to change my destination to a city that is to the east of my present location, I cannot merely *adjust* my heading. I must "repent"—turn around. I must take the next available exit and go in a completely different direction.

GPS systems are great for driving in unfamiliar territory. You enter the destination address, the system determines the best route, and off you go. If you divert from the programmed route, a voice will say, "Recalculating." Directions to get you back on the correct route to your destination will follow. While using a GPS, there are times that you may decide to diverge from the prescribed route, and it can be very aggravating to keep hearing the voice, "Recalculating." We start yelling at the voice, "Enough already!"

This is the way it can be when our own will comes in conflict with the direction Jesus wants us to go. Prevailing culture, Western or otherwise, can be profoundly hostile to the Jesus way of life and kingdom of God thinking. Ours is a culture that constantly promotes an agenda of entitlement, personal gratification, safety, security, comfort, and convenience. This mindset is at extreme odds with the agenda of the humble Master. Jesus modeled and taught a lifestyle of letting others go first, daily seeking to dispense mercy and grace, and picking up the towel of the servant to do the most menial of duties when the opportunity arises. In a word, it totally flies in the face of the idea of upward mobility and the *right to the pursuit of happiness.* Too often, as with the GPS, we choose our own direction and tune out the voice that keeps telling us we are off course.

Over and over again, we find the kingdom ethos to be counterintuitive. "The first will be last, and the last will be first." "Those who save their lives will lose them, and those who lose their lives for my sake, will discover them." Jesus is telling us that the source of abundant life and the purest form of joy lies in following his lead regarding how we disperse (spend) our lives. This is fundamental to what it really means for Jesus to be our Lord.

To live in the realm of the extraordinary means we take seriously the mandate of kingdom citizenship as taught and modeled by Jesus. We yoke ourselves to Jesus himself, submitting to his directives and authority for our lives. Fuller Theological Seminary professor George Ladd sheds light on this idea: "While Israel as a whole, including both leaders and people, refused to accept Jesus' offer of the Kingdom, a substantial group did respond in faith. Discipleship to Jesus was not like discipleship to a Jewish rabbi. The rabbis bound their disciples not to themselves but to the Torah: Jesus bound his disciples to himself. The rabbis offered something outside of themselves: Jesus offered himself alone. Jesus required his disciples to surrender without reservation to his authority."[8]

One of the prime biblical metaphors for the church is the *body* of Christ. This speaks to the idea of followers of Christ as occupying the position and responsibility of being flesh and blood containers and agents of Jesus' love, mercy, goodness, and works. So, our perception of the gospel must be that it not only provides a salvation that leads to security in post-death life, but it also transforms or redeems our earthly life and extends the kingdom of God throughout our world. We close this chapter with the profound words of *The Message* author Eugene Peterson in his take on Romans 12:1–2:

> So here's what I want you to do, God helping you: Take your everyday, ordinary life—your sleeping, eating, going-to-work, and walking-around life—and place it before God as an offering. Embracing what God does for you is the best thing you can do for him. Don't become so well-adjusted to your culture that you fit into it without even thinking. Instead, fix your attention on God. You'll be changed from the inside out. (Message)

>>> **2**

# MEET THE EXTRAS

*The Habit of Beholding Others*

> They set us up, and then we waited for them to set the
> equipment. Where I was standing, I could tell I was out
> of the picture, or at least way in the background.
>
> —Journal entry of a television extra

All movies and television shows have them. They are peripheral to the *real* action and focus of the camera, which is on the star or main characters, and you don't know their names, backgrounds, or body of work. You've probably never seen them before and most likely will never see them again. They are referred to as *extras*; basically they are human scenery. These are the people who sit at the tables in restaurant scenes looking as if they are chatting; they play the role of passersby on the sidewalk and the ones who are felled or blown up in battle scenes.

In the BBC series *Extras*, Ricky Gervais portrays the struggling Andy Millman, a wannabe actor who spends the majority of his waking moments on movie sets, stroking egos in hopes of being "discovered." Scheming, even begging, for movie lines or positions in scenes that place him in the camera viewfinder fills his days.

Just about anyone can play the part of an extra because extras are the nobodies of the acting world. They are necessary though, because a scene would be incomplete without them. It just wouldn't look or feel completely natural or believable if they were not present. But the focus of the camera is always the focus of the story line—the star(s) of the show. Extras are interchangeable parts who come and go with less than little fanfare.

Our own lives are filled to overflowing with "extras." Each and every day as we venture from the seclusion of our homes, we encounter them. The lady pumping gas in the next stall, the construction workers eating lunch on the tailgate of their pickup, the elderly gentleman pushing the shopping cart along the bread aisle. These are common examples of those we pass by and intermingle with every day, paying virtually no attention to. They are but background scenery to the main story line, which is my life, *my* story, and my agenda. Author and pastor Randy Frazee describes a common scenario:

> When the Johnsons go out for routine errands, they seldom encounter or relate to actual, real live people anymore. They get gas at a station where there is no attendant. Bob just sticks his credit card in the automated machine, fills up his gas tank, and takes off, not speaking to a single person in the process. Like most banking experiences these days, the Johnsons' experience is an automated one. When the Johnsons venture out to the large mall fifteen minutes away, they find themselves surrounded by a multitude of people, but they know no one. People seem to work hard at avoiding conversation.[1]

The question we need to ask is how things could be changed if we were to cultivate the habit of opening ourselves to the voice of the Holy Spirit. What if we took our cues from him, allowing the extras to intersect our lives and move into the deeper recesses of our consciousness—to intentionally help them taste and see the goodness of Jesus? Mother Teresa claimed this as her secret for dealing with the masses of broken and literally dying humanity she faced each day in the slums of Calcutta. When asked how she managed to avoid being overwhelmed by the deluge, she said, "I don't see crowds, I see individuals."

This was the very modus operandi of Jesus as he moved among throngs of people seeking healing and miracles. Seeing a funeral procession, his eyes moved through the denseness of the mourners to settle upon the broken and weeping mother of the young boy being carried away for burial. On another occasion as he was surrounded by pressing crowds, his eyes focused on a man in a tree whom he knew needed an encounter with him. At yet another time his gaze zeroed in on one particular tax collector, one of the most despised professions in Jewish culture at the time. Jesus invited this man named Levi (later called Matthew) to follow him as a disciple.

Most of us are so familiar with these stories that in our mind's eye we have no problem seeing these people as indi-

**JUST SAYIN'. . .**

If relationship is the key medium in the transfer of the gospel, then this simply means we are going to have to have meaningful connections with the people in our circle. Our very lives are our messages, and we cannot take ourselves out of the equation of mission. One of the profound implications of our being ambassadors of Jesus is that people get the idea that Jesus actually likes to hang out with them precisely because we do as his representatives. Through our friendship and attentiveness, they really do get the message that God loves them.

—*Alan Hirsch*

## JUST SAYIN'...

This is leading us into the issue commonly known by the Latin term *imago Dei*, which means "the image of God." To believe in the *imago Dei* is not to ignore or bypass the inherent sinfulness of all people. But it means that in spite of the fall of humankind through sin, every human being remains created and stamped with the fingerprint of God himself. The facts of this matter are central to what sets us apart from all other living creatures. Though the hands of God lovingly and carefully created animals, such as dogs, horses, and chimpanzees, they are not created in the image of God, as is humankind. When we encounter another human being, regardless of their spiritual state, we are encountering the handiwork of God that bears his very image. As Michael and I said in our book *ReJesus*, "To disregard the *imago Dei* in certain peoples is to treat them like animals. You never see Jesus doing that. Lepers, prostitutes, tax collectors, children, demoniacs—they were treated with great grace and respect by him."[2]

—*Alan Hirsch*

viduals. What we tend to forget is that they were each part of a dusty, eddying throng of people in a densely populated scene. The reason these three biblical characters stand out is because Jesus' listening ear to the voice of his Father, coupled with eyes that sought to see what the Father might want to show him beyond the ordinary, drew these individuals out of the crowd and set them on the center stage of Jesus' personal story.

## Summing Up People

The Gospels are replete with stories of Jesus' encounters with people he refused to simply pass by or *sum up* too quickly—something we all tend to do. This happens subconsciously in all of us in literal seconds as we see people in shops, on sidewalks, in restaurants, or even in photographs. Our minds quickly judge what a person is like, what their motives are, and if there is anything for us to gain by pursuing a deeper engagement with them. Studies reveal, "Certain brain regions are geared to pick up cues about other people on a first impression—with just a little information and maybe a few preconceived notions. Snap judgments, it turns out, aren't arbitrary at all, but are informed by what we see and know of our opinions about what certain personality traits suggest."[3]

Utilizing functional magnetic resonance imaging, researchers at New York University and Harvard scanned the brains of people "as they formed first impressions of fictional individuals based on simple descriptions and value representations."[4] The results revealed "considerable activity in the amygdala and posterior cingulate cortex regions of the brain during the 'encoding' period of information that was relevant to impression formation." The researchers' conclusion was that people unwittingly draw impressions "based on ambiguous and complex information but still, we're able to judge quickly how we feel about other people, and the ability to do this is due to the innate abilities of various brain regions." Consider the following from additional studies:

> Psychologists agree that snap judgments are a holistic phenomenon in which clues (mellifluous voice, Rolex watch, soggy handshake, hunched shoulders) hit us all at once and form an impression larger than their sum. Just three seconds are sufficient to make a conclusion about fresh acquaintances. . . .
>
> Nalini Ambady, professor of psychology at Tufts University in Medford, Massachusetts, studies first impressions carved from brief exposure to another person's behavior, what she calls "thin slices" of experience. She says humans have developed the ability to quickly decide whether a new person will hurt or enrich us—judgments that had lifesaving ramifications in an earlier era.
>
> She believes that thin slices are generated in the most primitive area of the brain, where feelings are also processed, which accounts for the emotional punch of some first encounters. Immediate distrust of a certain car salesman or affinity for a prospective roommate originates in the deepest corners of the mind.[5]

As Jesus' ambassadors, seeking to have a *right here, right now* impact, it is imperative that we cultivate in ourselves the Jesus habit of moving past prejudiced assessments of others we get via these initial impressions. We should work to develop a hearing ear and seeing eye to what the Lord is saying to us about another individual. A good example of this is found in the beginning of Jesus' encounter with the young man commonly referred to as the rich ruler.

### Beholding Others

> Then Jesus beholding him loved him.
>
> Mark 10:21 KJV

Contextually this verse occurs shortly after this wealthy young man has approached Jesus and asked him how he might obtain eternal life. Jesus begins to iterate the Ten Commandments, and the young man may have interrupted Jesus, saying he has kept them since his childhood. It is at this point that verse 21 says, "Then Jesus *beholding him* loved him" (KJV, our emphasis). This phrase is hugely important for us to grasp, or rather be grasped by. The word "beholding" is a Greek word used in astronomy for the study of the constellations. It means something way deeper than simply noticing or glancing at. There is much deeper intensity involved in the *looking*. Thayer's lexicon provides this definition:

Beholding
1. to have (the power of) understanding
2. to discern mentally, observe, perceive, discover, understand
3. to turn the thoughts or direct the mind to a thing, to consider, contemplate, to look at, to weigh carefully, examine[6]

The basic definition of the word "beholding" here means *to look at something in order to learn about it*. It evokes the idea of sincere and undivided attention that encapsulates the object of attention into the mind and complete consideration of the viewer.

Recently my wife and I were sitting on our back patio, enjoying the midnight cool and easy conversation, when we noticed a couple of shooting stars, which is always a thrill. The next morning we read in the news that the earth was in the midst of a particular meteor shower over a three-day period. That evening our teenage children joined us in the backyard, lying faceup on sleeping bags with focused attention on the night sky. In a matter of less than an hour, we witnessed dozens of shooting stars, each greeted with *oohs*, *aahs*, and *wows*! According to the meteorologists, the same general number of meteors fell the night before. The difference in our two evenings under the night sky was that one night we were just there passively *noticing*, the next night we were intentionally *beholding* the constellations. The biggest difference between the two nights was not what was happening in the sky but the attention we gave to the sky.

When Jesus "beheld" this young man, he was considering everything about him, not just what he saw with his eyes and heard with his ears. Jesus was looking for and seeing something much deeper than someone who was angst ridden and just wanted to make sure his eternal security was in place. This was what he could see on the surface. But Jesus always looked beyond the surface. He was listening to the voice of the Holy Spirit. Jesus was focused more on what the Father was saying about this young man than what the young man himself was saying.

The words used here by the Gospel writer were chosen carefully. He wanted us to know Jesus expressed his love by *beholding* the young man. This was a key part of "seeking and saving the lost," the very purpose he declared he was on earth for (Luke 19:10). For Jesus was constantly beholding people in this manner. Scan the Gospels and we witness many examples of this. Jesus' encounters with Zaccheus,

**JUST SAYIN'...**

If we are truly committed to bringing Jesus as the center of our lives among others and to see the church renewed in the mission of God, we will lead it toward a greater respect for the unbeliever, a greater grace for those who, though they don't attend church services, are nonetheless marked by God's image. It will lead to a greater respect for people in general.

—*Alan Hirsch*

the woman at the well, widows, soldiers, and children—all reveal an intentional self-pacing and rapt attention to people he came upon in "chance" encounters. He didn't see crowds, he saw individuals.

*I See You*

As we work to develop our hearts missionally, we should be encouraged by the fact that with practice any of us can cultivate the habit of beholding others and moving them from being *extras* in "our" story to becoming recipients of God's goodness and kindness on scales both large and small. In fact it is important to point out that living missionally is the sum total of both small and larger acts of reaching out.

Bestselling author Peter Senge points out the importance of seeing others that is found in the traditional greeting of a tribal people. "Among the tribes of northern Natal in South Africa, the most common greeting, equivalent to 'hello' in English, is the expression: *Sawu bona*. It literally means, 'I see you.' If you are a member of the tribe, you might reply by saying *Sikhona*, 'I am here.' The order of the exchange is important: until you see me, I do not exist. It's as if, when you see me, you bring me into existence."[7]

The present discontinuity and lack of integration of life in the twenty-first century has produced a society of strangers who seldom "see" one another. We will go deeper into the issue of estrangement and fragmentation in the chapters ahead, but it is important for us to consider here that our contemporary culture fosters a feeling of insignificance among others. For example, I find myself wondering if the fascination of Twitter and Facebook is mistakenly conceived as simple unabashed narcissism but is actually (at least in part) a cry of "Please see me, I am here, and I exist!" When people are tweeting and Facebooking their every move ("Sitting on the patio, enjoying iced tea and the dogs playing"), you have to wonder if there is a bit of loneliness going on. As technology has increased, the overall effect has not only failed to draw us closer but has actually spawned breeches in community and a breakdown of authentic social fabric coupled with a broad sense of isolation and loneliness for people, although their daily lives are spent in the midst of others. Michael Schluter and David Lee wrote a wonderful book on relational dynamics in the West. They say:

> Of all the changes accompanying industrial development, probably the most significant from the standpoint of encounter is that the scale of community we relate to has expanded beyond recognition. As a villager almost anywhere in twelfth-century Europe you would have known a limited number of people very well simply because you were stuck with them. It is difficult to imagine in the age of the car just how much isolation results from having to go places on foot—the nearest town becomes equivalent of a hundred-mile drive. Not surprisingly, therefore, pre-industrial communities tended to be self-sufficient, the village blacksmith and the village baker providing the nearest and most convenient source of their respective services as perhaps only the village pub does today. Everybody knew everybody else; everybody relied on everybody else.[8]

For us as God's missional people, being sent with a redemptive agenda, it is important that we understand and take into account the nature of contemporary culture, considering how we might be salt and light in the midst of an alienated and bored society of strangers. Behind the eyes of many people we brush past on a typical day is a soul who is seeking relationship and connection with others, and in many (if not most) cases a conscious or unconscious search for God. Schluter and Lee point out the barriers we face in this culture of strangers:

> In the West, we find ourselves scattered too far and moving too fast to maintain a strong base of encounter relationships. Relationship is less and less a matter of sharing the same patch of earth and the same block of air. We meet many more people, but less frequently; we still have friends and families, but on the whole these relationships are fewer, more intermittent, less stable. Instead we feel millions of tiny threads tying us into general and indirect relationship with people we will never touch or talk to, people who as individuals we know nothing about, nor ever will. And this has a profound effect on the way we live. For it means that in the mega-community we live among strangers.[9]

### Do Talk to Strangers

The Old Testament is replete with direct instructions from God on the treatment of strangers, and Jesus addressed it as well. The social impact that comes from being a *stranger* or the new kid on the block is a bitter pill to swallow for beings created in the image of God. Westerners have perfected the art of avoiding encounters with strangers. It is not uncommon for two individuals to pass on a sidewalk or in the halls of a hotel or office complex, brushing within a foot or so of one another, without speaking or acknowledging one another whatsoever. This deliberate avoidance of engaging strangers is really remarkable when we pause to consider it. Now, no doubt, if you live in New York City or ride a subway or train on your daily commute, it would be virtually impossible to speak to everyone you come along. But you get the idea. For the most part we live in a culture that doesn't even *try* to be friendly or engaging.

A few years ago a young couple relocated to the suburban home next door to my family. They moved in on a weekend when we were away so we were not able to welcome them or extend greetings as they were moving furniture into the house. The entire week went by without us having a chance to meet our new neighbors because I would be on the way to my office early in the morning and I noticed that the husband didn't return home from his job until late in the evening. I thought I would get a chance to say "hi" by the weekend.

The following Saturday morning, I heard a lawn mower running in the front yard, and I peeked out the window and saw my new neighbor mowing his front lawn. "Perfect," I thought, "I'll run out and finally introduce myself and welcome him to the neighborhood." I walked to the side of my front lawn and stood, waiting to catch his attention. As he turned the lawn mower and headed back in my direction, I was pretty sure that his eyes quickly darted toward and back away from me, but although he was headed straight for me, he did not look up. I figured that he was going to just come closer to me and shut off his mower and exchange greetings.

No dice. He got to within about three feet of me and I thought he was going to run me over before he stopped, turned, and headed for his next pass with the lawn mower. Thinking to myself, "Maybe he just possibly—I don't know how. Naw, no way. But I'll give him the benefit of the doubt—may have not noticed me." I sidestepped over to where his next pass would bring him. This happened three times, with me standing there, coffee cup in hand, most likely looking (and definitely feeling) pretty foolish. It became a cat-and-mouse game.

My new neighbor would come to the end of his yard, with me an arm's length away, in front of him. He would turn around and head away. I would step over a couple of feet and the whole thing would happen again. I finally slinked back into the house, pretty sure I had just entered bizarro world. A few days later I was able to finally corner the guy as he was watering his lawn—he was a nice fellow, just somewhat shy.

We have become experts at avoiding interaction with strangers. Just check out the seating situation the next time you are in an

## JUST SAYIN'...

Middle-class culture strives to protect and maintain its sense of privacy as it seeks more and more security, convenience, and comfort. Learning to live as missionaries in such a culture means that Christians will have to break from the very same propensity and step out of the privatized comfort zones we have created for ourselves if we harbor any hope of creating missional communities.

— *Alan Hirsch*

airport as people wait to board an airplane and you will notice that some people have gone to great measures to keep from having another person sit next to them by stuffing chairs with luggage, laptop computers, or newspapers. In movie theaters people will settle for a seat that is offset from the center of the screen if it ensures that they will not be forced to sit next to a stranger. A year-old issue of the *Cross Stitching Almanac* in a doctor's office waiting room will gain our unbridled attention if it will occupy the uncomfortable air in a roomful of strangers and ease the tension caused by not acknowledging them or engaging in conversation. Brennan Manning notes our propensity to avoid those on the margins of our attention as well as Jesus' words on the matter:

> There exists a problem of epic biblical proportions: I've divided the human community into certain categories. There are a few people whom I like, and a multitude whom I seldom think about, move proactively toward, or manifest any concern for. Yet the evangelical witness described in Matthew and Luke quashes discrimination of any kind. "If all you do is love the lovable, do you expect a bonus?" Jesus asks. "Anybody can do that. If you simply say hello to those who greet you, do you expect a medal? Any run-of-the-mill sinner can do that" (Matt. 5:46–47, The Message). Any of us can love someone with whom we have a mutual interest or attraction. I find it effortless to turn on to people who favor my existence and make me feel good. So did the contemptible tax-collectors, traitors to the Jewish cause.[10]

## Smile and the Whole World Smiles with You

My wife, Sherri, would be the first to admit that she is by nature a shy person, but several years ago she purposely focused on developing the habit of *seeing* others as she shopped for groceries by greeting them with a smile and a "hi." This became a practice and for her a genuine spiritual discipline, as she consciously trained herself to be friendly, complimentary, or initiating conversation when the opportunity presented itself. For several years now Sherri has engaged herself in the practice of purposely sharing greetings and smiles while she shops. Not to overstate the matter, but a routine, even mundane or dreaded chore has now become a mission of friendliness, requiring nothing more than a willing participant to initiate the exchange.

According to researchers, expressions are contagious, be they happy, angry, sad, or smiling. It is difficult for us to remain expressionless. Swedish researchers concluded the unconscious mind usurps power over our facial muscles. The leaders of the study

> told volunteers to react to a series of pictures of expressionless, happy or angry faces. They were told to make frowning, smiling or expressionless faces in return. Often the face they were told to attempt was the opposite of what might be expected—meeting a smile with a frown, or a frown with a smile. Movements in their facial muscles were measured using equipment that picked up electrical signals from the fibers. However, the results showed that volunteers simply did not have total control over their facial muscles. While it was easy to frown back at a picture of an angry man, it was much more difficult to pull a smile. Even though study subjects were trying consciously to curb their natural reactions, the twitching in their muscles told a different story. [The lead doctor] describes this as "emotional contagion."[11]

Recently two students from Purdue University took it upon themselves to grab a spot on the college campus each week to give away free compliments to anyone who wanted one. The pair

**JUST SAYIN'...**

We are called to be a community of holiness. This is not about moral standards but an issue that points to the saving work of Jesus on our behalf. The kingdom fruit of kindness, gentleness, peace, and goodness are not an issue of our gaining God's favor. The beauty is that they are in truth the fruit of God's favor and grace through the cross, and these are the values that should underscore the difference in the lives of Jesus' followers from the surrounding culture.

—*Alan Hirsch*

drew widespread notoriety from entities such as National Public Radio, *Good Morning America*, and even an appearance on *Oprah*. They eventually went on a tour of several major cities, spreading the *compliment gospel*. Brett Westcott and Cameron Brown are now commonly known as The Compliment Guys. On one hand it is a sad commentary on our culture when we realize how rare friendliness and nicety actually is, but on the flip side is the positive realization of how simple it is to live out some of the genuinely missional ways of behaving. It should cause the Christian community serious pause though, if we are willing to be honest and realize that the contemporary church is not typically viewed as the bringer of good news, smiles, and compliments.

Three recent books speak to this malady: *UnChristian* by David Kinnaman and Gabe Lyons, Dan Kimball's *They Like Jesus but Not the Church*, and Dan Merchant's *Lord Save Us from Your Followers* all relate a litany of interviews and exchanges with non-Christians that perceive Christians and the church as being negative and judgmental in tone and demeanor. We encourage our readers to decide today to change your parcel of influence and be a smile giver throughout your day-to-day travels.

### People of Shalom

How lovely on the mountains
Are the feet of him who brings good news,

Who announces peace
And brings good news of happiness,
Who announces salvation,
And says to Zion, "Your God reigns!"

Isaiah 52:7 NASB

If we are known for anything, we Christians should be known as people of peace; that wherever we traverse, peace emits from us. In what most scholars agree was one of Jesus' most central teachings, he proclaimed, "Blessed are the peacemakers, for they will be called children of God" (Matt. 5:9 NRSV). Jesus himself said that one of the key distinguishing features that marks us as the children of God will be peace. In another passage, the apostle Paul encourages, "If it is possible, as far as it depends on you, live at peace with everyone" (Rom. 12:18). Think about that. What would happen if every place you were to go to today, as far as it depends on you, peace would be manifest?

Peace is a consistent theme throughout the New Testament, and Paul continually refers to the Lord as "the God of peace" (Rom. 15:33; 16:20; 1 Cor. 14:33) and the church as the benefactors and carriers of that same peace. In short, we *are* the people of God's Shalom. Our lives—the way we conduct ourselves—should give off the scent of peace. This is a key fruit of the Spirit we should be feeding to the world.

Unfortunately, peace is not the most common element found in Christians. One morning I was having coffee with a friend who was a pastor from my area. As our conversation moved to the subject of raising and developing disciples of Jesus who can transform a local community, he shook his head and frowned, saying, "Disciples? I can't even get my people to be nice to each other." It reminded me of the famous rant by Jim Mora, coach of the Indianapolis Colts, following a disappointing loss where his team played very poorly. An unfortunate reporter asked Mora about his team's chances of success in the approaching playoffs and was met with a

95

flabbergasted and irritated response. "Playoffs?! Don't talk about playoffs! You kiddin' me?! Playoffs?! I just hope we can win a game!" My pastor friend had difficulty imagining his church as a village of disciples because the reality was, they couldn't even get the "peace" thing down—something so fundamental to the faith.

In our quest to carry out a faithful mission as God's ambassadors, we should honestly evaluate our "peace" quotient. We should consider whether or not we evoke peace in our daily interactions with others and make a point of "so far as it depends on *us*, be at peace with all men." The Word of God commands us to *pursue* peace (2 Tim. 2:22; 1 Peter 3:11), and one can only imagine the results if we who claim the sign of the cross placed as much thought and effort into cultivating peace as we do in justifying ourselves and criticizing others.

### Creative Grace

> Use your heads as you live and work among outsiders. Don't miss a trick. Make the most of every opportunity. Be gracious in your speech. The goal is to bring out the best in others in a conversation, not put them down, not cut them out.
>
> Colossians 4:5–6 Message

Todd Hunter, pastor and Anglican bishop, provides an excellent exegesis of this passage as he unpacks the key phrases in it, pointing out "that faith in and following Jesus spreads as the cooperative friends of Jesus live in creative goodness for the sake of others through the animating and empowering presence of the Holy Spirit."[12]

> • *Use your heads.* This means that we should be present and alert to our life, to God and to the people and events of our life. . . .

- *As you live and work among outsiders.* ... Paul reminded [the Colossians] that the normal routines of life, the people and events that make our communities, matter. These are spiritual. We don't need to add "spiritual" activities to our life as much as we need to make our actual, everyday life spiritual. ...
- *Don't miss a trick. Make the most of every opportunity.* Here Paul encourages us to live constant lives of creative goodness. We don't want to miss any opportunity; even small things matter. ...
- *Be gracious in your speech.* What is gracious speech? It is others-oriented. It asks, What will these words do to my hearer? Gracious speech seeks the good of others. ...
- *The goal is to bring out the best in others.* We act and speak for the sake of others with the goal that they'll know we are interested in their good. ...
- *In a conversation.* Respect—listening to others, really hearing them, connecting with what they are saying even if we do not agree—is at the heart of this passage. ...
- *[Do] not put them down, [do] not cut them out.* The growing hostility toward Christians is very much a reflection of what outsiders feel they receive from believers. They say their aggression simply matches the oversized opinions and egos of Christians.[13]

As we consider what it means to *behold* others in the spirit and manner of Jesus, it may help to think in terms of what it means to socially place our arm around the shoulders of those we come across. This practice of embracing others with genuine attention and otherly focused concern can only come about by investing the mental energy and spiritual listening necessary to get beyond surface appearances.

## From the Mouth of Babes

Have you ever been rebuked by a four-year-old? A few years back I was standing on the sidewalk in front of a small bicycle shop as the owner was testing a new bike I had just purchased. He was making adjustments to the brakes and riding it up and down the side street after each change to the settings. Standing alongside me was his little girl. She had not uttered a word and seemed concerned about nothing beyond the lollipop in her mouth and the doll clutched in her arms.

Trying to make conversation as we both stood watching her father on the bicycle passing by, I said, "Your dad is the bike man, isn't he?" That simple statement jolted this little girl out of her silence. I had just awakened a sleeping giant. With a "pop," she pulled the sucker out of her mouth, looked up at me through squinted eyes, and declared, "He's not the bike man! He's *Daddy* man!" Needless to say, I was left speechless.

Her message could not have been clearer: "Dude, you have no clue. Don't you dare minimize my dad and think you know him based on the limited vision and petty thought you have put into it. You are summing his value up in terms of his vocation and what you see him *do*, not based on who he *is*. The fact of the matter is that he is my provider, my protector, and my hero! You just don't get it, do you?"

I had just been *schooled* by a four-year-old on what it means to *behold* someone.

— IDEAS AND SUGGESTIONS FOR FORMING A MISSIONAL LIFESTYLE —

*Pray—*

- Before leaving your home for the day, ask the Lord to open your eyes and heart to those along your path. Ask

the Holy Spirit to alert you to opportunities to engage strangers with the goodness of Jesus.
- Pray to see the *imago Dei* (the image of God) in people and to see them as God does.

*Practice*—

- Be a smile-maker. Cultivate the habit of smiling and greeting others every time you have the opportunity. Smile at your waitress, your cashier, etc. You may want to place some smiley-face stickers in your car and places around your house as a reminder to *smile*.
- Be a peacemaker. Speak a good word in the midst of tense situations.

*Welcome new neighbors*—

- Take some baked goods to new neighbors as they are moving in or shortly thereafter.
- Invite their children to play with your kids.
- Host a "welcome to the neighborhood" dinner party and invite the new neighbors and a few established neighbors to attend.

*Take inventory*—

- At the end of your day, consider specific moments as to how you viewed the people you came into contact with. Did you "behold" others or view them as scenery?

»»» **3**

# FROM PAPER TO PAVEMENT

*Believing and Being the Gospel*

> The Pharisees were religious students. They consumed
> the old covenant Law and thrived on it. They could
> quote it verbatim, interpret it and explain its fine points.
> They could do anything except live it!
>
> Malcolm Smith

After leaving work on a chilly February night in the
Bronx, New York, thirty-one-year-old social worker
Julio Diaz followed a daily routine as he hopped off
the subway to head to his favorite diner for his evening meal.
The platform appeared empty as he approached the stairs
leading to the street, and he hardly noticed the teenage boy
stepping from the shadows to confront him, knife in hand.
With the young man demanding money, Julio pulled out his
wallet and handed it over.

Something extraordinary happened next. As the boy began walking away, Diaz hollered to him, "Hey, wait a minute. You forgot something. If you're going to be robbing people for the rest of the night, you might as well take my coat to keep you warm." The awestruck teenager couldn't believe his ears, and a few minutes later the two of them were sharing a warm meal at Julio's favorite diner, where the youngster not only returned Julio's wallet but handed him his holdup knife as well. The conversation at the diner was dominated by the young man's questions as to why Julio was so nice to everyone. "Even the dishwasher." The answer is that Julio had incarnated Jesus' words:

Love your enemies. Let them bring out the best in you, not the worst. When someone gives you a hard time, respond with the energies of prayer for that person. If someone slaps you in the face, stand there and take it. If someone grabs your shirt, giftwrap your best coat and make a present of it. If someone takes unfair advantage of you, use the occasion to practice the servant life. No more tit-for-tat stuff. Live generously. (Luke 6:27–30 Message)

The late John Wimber was known for holding a Bible up and saying, "This is the menu, folks . . . it ain't the meal." Wimber was right. In many ways the Bible is very much like a menu. It only becomes a full-course meal when we add the ingredients of our lives to it and allow it to take over our mind, will, and body. When we mix the Word of God with real feet-to-the-pavement living, we can experience a kingdom feast every day and invite others to join us at that table. Until we let this happen, the words of the Bible remain as dormant as garden seeds left in their original envelope. The words just languish as possibilities, ideas, and options.

The apostle John gives instructions in the simplest phrase possible, "Whoever claims to live in him must walk as Jesus did" (1 John 2:6). In the words of a friend, "It ain't rocket surgery." It is not about trying to *do* what Jesus would do. Rather, it has to do with *thinking* the way Jesus thinks in order to live the way Jesus lived. Dallas Willard said, "Another important way of putting this is to say that I am learning from Jesus to live *my* life as he would live my life if he were I. I am not necessarily learning to do everything he did, but I am learning how to do everything I do in the manner that he did all that he did."[1] Therefore it's not so much about WWJD? (What Would Jesus Do?) but rather WIJD? (What Is Jesus Doing?). Being people of the Good News is about *seeing* people, things, and situations the way Jesus sees them and responding as he would if he were in our shoes.

We should seriously consider how we treat the telemarketer who upsets us by calling at dinnertime. We should ask, "How is Jesus in me wanting to deal with this person? It is about treating a waiter or waitress the way Jesus would, or helping out a struggling next-door neighbor the way the Word of God speaks to treating a neighbor. This is simply but profoundly about *being* the way Jesus is. It is about *driving* our cars with patience and courtesy in the same way Jesus would drive. That very thought is something we all should chew on. In fact, when I was pastoring, someone in our church wanted to have bumper stickers printed with the name of our church on them. I told this person I wouldn't stand for it, because I had seen some of our people (myself included) in traffic. It would have made for bad advertising.

Reading the Bible is as much about letting the Bible read us as it is about us reading it. "For the word of God is living and active. Sharper than any double-edged sword, it penetrates even to dividing soul and spirit, joints and marrow; it judges the thoughts and attitudes of the heart" (Heb. 4:12). This can only happen by coming to the Bible in a dialogical posture, not reading it as if it were a monological stone tablet. We should sit down with the Word of God as we would with a close friend or confidant, sharing conversation and coffee. The power of Scripture comes to life when we give ourselves to its message in the real living of our lives, letting it analyze us even more than we analyze it. Alan and coauthor Mike Frost say it well here:

> Any conversation must allow for both sides to communicate, and this most unfamiliar act is allowing oneself to be open to hearing God speak. One of the biases that we bring to the Bible, and one that blocks the possibility of true conversation, is the assumption that we read it. We are the active party. The Jewish approach to Scripture is that we don't read the Bible but rather that it reads us! Our standard practice is to assume we are its interpreter and therefore the arbiter of its meaning. Jewish approaches reverse this: we are not the interpreter, but rather it is the Torah that interprets us. This is because it is God who addresses us in Scripture; hence the idea of revelation that is so important to a biblical worldview. "It is not so much that we raise questions about him, but that he raises questions of us."[2]

This has a transformative effect on us as we take consistent doses to renew our thoughts to the mind of Christ. This is a change from *feeding on* to *fellowshipping with* the Word of God. It consistently has a power to calibrate thought processes to the thinking pattern of the Lord, but it is only activated when we act on it. Mere exposure to it does not change us into agents of the kingdom.

> Do not merely listen to the word, and so deceive yourselves. Do what it says. Anyone who listens to the word but does not

do what it says is like a man who looks at his face in a mirror and, after looking at himself, goes away and immediately forgets what he looks like. (James 1:22–24)

## Jesus Time

For as long as I can remember, I have had a routine like a lot of believers maintain where I spend a bit of time in the morning in the Bible and prayer. For me, there is usually a cup of coffee at hand, a groggy dog at foot, and a guitar nearby to spend a little time in praise and worship. It dawned on me a few years back that I had fallen into a pattern that in effect had me leaving Jesus in that *quiet-time corner* each morning as I embarked on my daily duties. It was as if I was saying, "Well, gotta' get goin'. Great hanging with you, Lord. See ya tomorrow." It had become somewhat routinized, and it was as if I was leaving Jesus in the book, bookmarked and all.

Now, consciously I was not intending to do that, but practically speaking that is exactly what I was doing. My daily Bible reading duty was checked off the list. It was much like the old-time Country and Western radio shows where thirty minutes of songs about drunkenness, fighting, and fornication would be interrupted as the host drew a serious tone and announced, "It's now *sacred time* on our show." Everything would slow down and what would follow would be a solemn old-time gospel song. As soon as it was over? *Bam!* Back to singing about bar fights and kickin' out the footlights. I felt that I was doing something like that . . . giving Jesus a daily token acknowledgment, then going about my own agenda and pursuits.

Consistently feeding on the Word of God is important, and in that regard my routine had great value. But something very positive happened when I realized how I was limiting the Lord in my life. This had to do with my approach to the Bible, the "why" of my purpose for reading it in the first place. It had become a type of daily booster shot—you know, a "chapter a day keeps the devil away." When I realized this, I began to approach the Bible with an aim of being transformed into a missional person who would live that day with a goal of incarnating the Word for others, of *being* good news wherever I went. I decided I would no longer leave Jesus stuck in the corner and on the pages of the book. It began to change everything.

Approaching the Bible in this way turns into a daily invitation for Jesus to join us in our routines. *My* day becomes *our* day when we seek to incarnate the Word in the here and now of our days and weeks. This, in a way, is letting our flesh become the Word. In my own walk I've made certain passages a "make this verse *flesh*" goal for each day. Verses such as, "Pleasant words are like a honeycomb, sweetness to the soul and health to the bones" (Prov. 16:24 NKJV) become a challenge to make them come alive. For me, it has become a goal to respond with healthy, pleasant, sweet-to-the-soul words to others—telemarketers and license bureau workers included. Notice I said that this is a *goal*. I am the first to admit that many days I fail, but it is one of my daily missional goals. Having a conscious challenge brings it into measurable focus.

This is the posture that Lesslie Newbigin commended when he said, "It is possible to indwell the Bible story so that you do not so much look *at* the Bible from without as look at the world from within the Bible, through the lenses that the Bible gives you."[3] This is another way of describing the adoption of a biblical *worldview*. Newbigin's suggestion takes the position of placing ourselves inside the Word and working our lives out from that position—like looking through a new set of glasses. As we read a section of Scripture, we think through how to contextualize it in our own lives.

So one of the questions we can ask ourselves each day as we read the Bible is, "What situations, people, or issues, in my life right now or where I will find myself today, are similar to what I have just read?" We then look for the appropriate actions, words, or response from the key players in that passage and think and pray through how we might live out the truth of the Word in our parcel of the world. This actually adds a bit of lab, or homework, to our Bible study.

## Sunday Schooled

Not long ago my teenage son and I were driving from St. Louis to Milwaukee when we stopped off for breakfast at a fast-food joint. It was a Sunday morning and the place was woefully understaffed. One poor guy was working the kitchen and there was a middle-aged woman covering both the front counter and the drive-thru. As we walked in, eyeing the situation, I whispered, "Uh oh." There were literally only two people working the early morn-ing breakfast rush. Between labored breaths and without looking up, the lady apologized to the half dozen or so of us who were in line and explained that two other workers had either called in sick or just failed to show up for work.

**JUST SAYIN'...**

Jewish philosopher Martin Buber spoke of the mistake so many scholars make. They objectify the Bible, turning it into ideology and head knowledge alone, moving from what he called an I-and-Thou stance toward an I-and-It relation to the Scriptures. When we objectify it in this way—when it effectively becomes an object, an "It"—we remain firmly in control and are not changed by encountering the living Word. People are not convinced by teaching but by encounter. Doctrine follows as a way of explaining the impact of the encounter.

—*Alan Hirsch*

Despite their hopeless situation, these two workers buzzed like bees and worked as hard and fast as humanly possible to serve a line of cars outside and a growing stream of custom-ers inside. Fortunately everyone in line was very patient and understanding of the situation, not laying blame on these two people who had faithfully shown up for work. Everyone, that is, except for one guy. Near the front of the line was a man who was probably in his middle fifties, dressed to the nines, and holding his Sunday school lesson in hand, obviously headed to church.

Shortly after placing his order, the guy was leaning on the counter, grunting, groaning, weight shifting from foot to foot, and watching every move of the two workers with steely eyes and pursed lips, as if they were handling the delivery of his firstborn. After a few minutes he literally shouted at the two desperate workers, "I would please like to have my food now so that I can get going!" With teary eyes and flushed cheeks, the lady working the counter maintained her composure and apologized for the delay, although it was obvious to everyone she was on the brink of a dam burst of tears and in the midst of an impossible situation. As this church-bound "saint" stomped out of the restaurant, the disgust of everyone else in the place was evident. Not a person said a word, but thought balloons were floating over everyone's head: "Jerk!" "What an ass." "Hypocrite." "Typical Christian." "Geeze—and the dude's goin' to church." It was clear to everyone where this guy was in such a hurry to get to.

After Sunday School Sam departed, the place was silent and the atmosphere was thick with an undercurrent of sadness rippled with anger. I did the only thing I knew to do at the moment and that was to voice appreciation to the two workers for their great effort. "You guys are doing great, I don't know how you're doing it, but I think you deserve a raise. Hopefully that guy meets Jesus when he gets to church!" This broke the tension, and a few other people pitched in their agreement to the affirmation, and like a person underwater for too long and finally breaking the surface, the lady at the counter let out a sigh of relief and gave a thankful smile.

It was easy. I just seized the opportunity to live out the verse from Proverbs that I had been focusing on—"Pleasant words are like a honeycomb, sweetness to the soul and health to the bones." The atmosphere had instantly changed. I thought at any moment munchkins were going to jump out and start singing, "The witch is dead, the wicked, wicked witch is dead!"

This is not an isolated scenario. My two daughters worked at a fast-food restaurant, and their most dreaded day to work was Sundays because, they said, the most belligerent customers were the church folk. I still am not sure that is the case, but at the very least I know it seemed that way because they *expected* more out of Christians. Most of us who have known anyone in the restaurant business have heard that Christians are usually the least generous when it comes to tipping. The scenarios just described are very real examples of why Christians are not generally viewed as *good news people* by the general population. Too often, their actions and presence are old news or, even worse, bad news. Steve Sjogren seeks to counter this as he implores his flock to tip 25 percent in restaurants on Sundays as a missional practice/discipline. Imagine the impact we can make by doing the same and focusing always on being God's good news people in restaurants, cafés, and any place we shop. Brennan Manning says:

> In the last analysis, faith is not the sum of our beliefs or a way of speaking or a way of thinking; it is a way of living and can be articulated adequately only in a living practice. To acknowledge Jesus as Savior and Lord is meaningful insofar as we try to live as he lived and to order our lives according to his values.[4]

Alan is fond of saying that the gospel is like a virus we sneeze on others. I know that might be a rather gross analogy, but it really is much like that. The gospel needs a host, a carrier, to get spread around. The power of the gospel is activated when we add our flesh and blood to it as Jesus did. Too often we quarantine it in our systems. Compartmentalizing Christian life into church attendance and church activity and between the covers of our Bibles is an incapacitating straitjacket that pervades Christianity. It not only limits our ability to get the message across; in many ways, it is counterproductive. It parks, or stores, the movement ethos that lies within the very message of the gospel in the first place. But as we allow the Word of God access to our hands, our lips, our time and resources, it is unleashed. It moves freely and powerfully into the streams of our daily lives and throughout neighborhoods and communities. And so we become God's good news people, giving Jesus the right to live through us right here, right now.

This is the very essence of what it means to have a missional approach to the Bible. As we study the Scripture, we ask, "How does God's Word call, shape, transform, and send me out into the world today?" We are praying, "Lord, I don't want to just read this passage and leave unchanged by it. Let me not just feed myself from this daily bread but help me feed others with it also."

### Feed Me

Pastors are aware that one of the common critiques uttered by Christians who leave their churches is "I just wasn't being fed." Any guy or gal who has been involved in leading a church for any amount of time has heard this countless times. This sentiment comes from the desire for more and better teaching, either in Bible studies or through better sermons. Many

Christians believe the inner hunger they feel will be satiated by more Bible study or through hearing sermons. They are convinced their spiritual strength or lack thereof is the responsibility of the pastor-preacher. I believe their hunger is very real, a gnawing lack of fulfillment and desire for more, but I do not believe it is for lack of teaching.

Several years ago, when the *Bible Code* book was the big buzz, from time to time church members would approach me and ask what I thought about the Bible code. I usually replied that I had not really given it *any* thought, but once we figured out how to live the *Gospel Code*, then we would look into it. My trite answer belies the fact that I am convinced that most of the books such as this not only fail to produce any substantive maturity in the body of Christ, they actually serve as diversionary devices to keep Christians mesmerized by anything other than the simple but rarely seen gospel-lived life. More knowledge and teaching is not going to do the trick . . . it is in living out the words of the Bible that the life of God begins to take root in us and spring up.

Jesus didn't say, "Come and *study* me." He said, "Come and *follow* me." It is through practicing what we study from the Bible in the laboratory of daily life that transformation happens in our own lives and we become a blessing to others. Bible study is not only important, it is absolutely vital and essential, and neither Alan nor I minimize its place in the daily rhythm of following Jesus. But the point here is that it is only the first step in feasting with the Lord on a daily basis, and just because we've studied something from the Bible doesn't mean the lesson is learned or complete. It has just begun.

## Believing in Jesus

In what is my favorite scene from *The Andy Griffith Show*, my favorite television series of all time, Opie, Andy Taylor's son, has been caught in an impossible-to-believe tale. The story line has Opie frequently coming home with various items such as a hand ax and an old quarter. When asked where he has acquired the items, he tells of Mr. McBeevee, a man who *walks in the treetops and wears a shiny silver hat, has twelve extra hands, blows smoke from his ears,* and *jingles when he walks.* Clearly Opie has dreamed up the mystical Mr. McBeevee in order to cover up the truth that he has actually stolen the ax and the money.

The most poignant scene in the episode has Andy attempting to pry the truth from his son as he sternly instructs Opie to simply confess that Mr. McBeevee is make-believe and all will be forgotten. The writer's script reads:

```
Opie makes a decision. He shrugs,
speaks in a weary monotone.

               OPIE
          Mr. McBeevee . . . is only
          make- . . .

               ANDY
             Say it.

Opie makes a difficult decision.

               OPIE
          I can't, Paw. Mr. McBeevee
          isn't make-believe. He's
          real.

Andy looks at the boy's upturned
face. Now comes the fateful
question.

               OPIE
             (continuing)
```

```
Don't you believe me?

Andy pauses. He wants to postpone
facing the all-important question.

              OPIE
        Don't you, Paw?

It's the moment of decision. Andy
is troubled. He looks at the earnest
face. Then the answer is there.
Andy's sternness relaxes. He finds
a strange peace within him as he
reaches out to take Opie's hand.

              ANDY
      I believe you.⁵
```

Andy leaves the boy in his room, slowly descends the stairs, and is met by his sidekick, Barney, who presses him on the need to punish Opie for what is an "obvious lie" by asking him if he himself believes in the far-fetched Mr. McBeevee. Andy lights a cigarette as he ponders the situation. Slowly and wistfully he says, "No . . . no . . . but I *do* believe in Opie."

In a last-ditch effort to make sense of it all, Andy goes out to the woods where Opie claims Mr. McBeevee walks in the treetops and ruefully says to no one in particular, "Mr. McBeevee." At this point a voice overhead answers, "Hello, somebody call?!" and Mr. McBeevee, a telephone company lineman, descends a tree, wearing a shiny hat, and with twelve tools hanging from his belt that jingle at the slightest move, puts out his hand, smiles, and gleefully greets Andy, "McBeevee at your service, what can I do for you?" Because of his unwavering belief in Opie, Andy just had to work out the answer to what seemed to be an unbelievable story. It wasn't enough to say, "I believe in Opie," and leave it at that. It was the very

**JUST SAYIN'...**

When referring to knowing God, the OT often uses the word *yada*. This word derives from the idea of personal intimacy between people and can be used to describe sexual intercourse. It refers to a deeply subjective form of knowledge where intellectual barriers are overcome and the immeasurable distance between knower and known is finally bridged: it approximates what the later mystics would call "union with God." Mere objective knowledge leaves the knower uncommitted, but truly knowing God, in the deepest biblical sense, can only be gained by a thoroughly personal, existential involvement, and through a self-giving that is rooted in the total self-giving which is the very life of God.

—*Alan Hirsch*

fact that Andy *did* believe in his son that pushed him to pursue the truth of Opie's words.

When we believe in someone, it means we believe in what they say and our actions prove that we do. You can't have one without the other. On the other hand, I can believe that a politician *exists*, but that doesn't necessarily mean I believe *in* the politician. I can believe that a car salesman exists but still not believe *in* him.

A lot of Christians demonstrate by their attitudes, actions, and interactions with others that they believe Jesus existed, but they fall way short of demonstrating that they *believe in* him. It is up to us to look at our pattern of day-to-day living and ask if our lives corroborate our stated belief *in* Jesus. Statistical studies consistently reveal no discernable difference in the way Christians live their lives in comparison to non-Christians. German theologian Johann Metz carries this thought further:

If we are to trust the gospel testimonies, it goes through people like a shock, reaching deep down into the direction their lives are taking, into their established system of needs, and so finally into the situations in society they have helped to create; it damages and disrupts one's own self-interests and aims at a fundamental revision of one's habitual way of life. The crisis (or sickness) of life in the church is not just that the change of heart is not taking place or not taking place quickly enough, but that the absence of this change of heart is being further concealed under the appearance of a merely *believed-in faith*. Are we Christians in this country really changing our hearts, or do we just believe in a change of hearts and remain under the cloak of this belief in conversion basically unchanged? Are we living as disciples, or do we just believe in discipleship and, under the cloak of this belief in discipleship, continue in our old ways, the same unchanging ways? Do we show real love, or do we just believe in love and under the cloak of belief in love remain the same egoists and conformists we have always been? Do we share the sufferings of others, or do we just believe in this sharing, remaining under the cloak of a belief in "sympathy" as apathetic as ever?[6]

## Believing Jesus

Do you just *believe in* Jesus or do you also *believe Jesus?* I ask this question neither rhetorically nor with cynicism but to point out the monumental difference between the two. If we harbor any realistic hope of making an impact on our world right here and right now, our lives must manifest the fruit of believing what Jesus said about how to live and love. Our intellectual and theological constructs fail miserably at bringing us into the freedom, glory, and power of the Word *made flesh*. Brennan Manning pulls no punches when he says:

> The problem with all this intellectualizing is that it allowed us to wrap the crucified Christ up in words. As we focused on theology, we separated ourselves from his humanity. We marked him only for our minds, so there was never any pressure in our guts to change our lives.[7]

It may be that we have actually placed more faith in the Bible than we have in Jesus. I fully believe in the inerrancy of the Bible, but I also believe that the majority of Christians today are bogged down in a Bible-faith that often stops short of a Jesus-faith. Robert Webber addresses it this way:

> The primary problem we evangelicals have inherited from the Enlightenment is its emphasis on the foundational nature of Scripture. The church has from its very beginning confessed that Jesus Christ is the foundation of faith: "No one can lay any foundation other than the one already laid, which is Jesus Christ" (1 Cor. 3:11). This foundation of Christianity is the incarnation of God into our humanity to do for us what we cannot do for ourselves: Defeat the powers of evil and restore the creation in the new heavens and the new earth. It was during the Enlightenment that the foundation of the Christian faith shifted from the centrality of the person and work of Jesus Christ to the centrality of the Bible. Theology shifted from the God who acts to the God who spoke. In the worst scenario faith shifted from trust in Christ to trust in the Book. Therefore, the first question we must address as evangelicals in a postmodern world is this: Do we believe in a book or a person?[8]

Jesus is the one who brought this issue up in the first place in one of his classic confrontations with a group of religious persecutors:

> You do not have His word abiding in you, for you do not believe Him whom He sent. You search the Scriptures because you think that in them you have eternal life; it is these that testify about Me; and you are unwilling to come to Me so that you may have life. (John 5:38–40 NASB)

Jesus made it very clear that it is possible to frequently go to the Bible and remain "unwilling to come to [him]." The Pharisees and leaders of the synagogues proved this. No one before or since could come close to matching the Pharisees' knowledge and devotion to the Scriptures. The real issue here has to do with *obeying* the Word. More study does not always lead to deeper obedience. Again, the menu isn't the meal. Studying the menu will not provide nourishment nor curb hunger. The twentieth-century martyr Dietrich Bonhoeffer said:

> Since he is the Christ, he must make it clear from the start that his word is not an abstract doctrine, but the re-creation of the whole life of man. The only right and proper way is quite literally to go with Jesus. The road to faith passes through obedience to the call of Jesus. Unless a definite step is demanded, the call vanishes into thin air, and if men imagine that they can follow Jesus without taking this step, they are deluding themselves like fanatics.[9]

### Just Think It?

When we speak of Jesus as the incarnation, we are agreeing with John's statement that Jesus was the Word of God made into flesh (John 1:14). This is the heart of our message as Christians, the belief that Jesus both fulfilled and reveals God's intention for humans and the world. He is the prototypical human being, and if people want to know how God feels about them, they should be able to listen and look to God's good news people giving life to his Word in order to get the right message.

Theologically thick words sometimes do more harm than good in conveying a meaning, but we may find them helpful on this point. Ortho*doxy* conveys the idea of *right thinking*. Ortho*praxy* speaks to the issue of *right action*. The globally successful Nike shoe campaign of years ago would have failed miserably if it had said, "Just Think It." "Just Do It" carried much more punch. As Alan and Mike conveyed in *The Shaping of Things to Come*, "It is our contention that by focusing on the development of the speculative doctrines, the early church lost the vital focus on the historical and practical implications of the faith. Mission and discipleship as such became marginal to theological correctness. Orthopraxy gave way to orthodoxy."[10]

## — Ideas and Suggestions for Forming a Missional Lifestyle —

*Pray—*

- During your morning or evening time in the Bible, pray the Lord will send you out in the Spirit of what you have read.

*Imagine—*

- Concentrate on what it means to "believe Jesus" in light of what you are facing today or this week. Think about the connection between your situation and how Jesus' words relate to it.

*Ask—*

- Formulate a set of questions to take with you to your reading of the Bible. A couple suggestions:
- "What would it look like in my life if I made these words *flesh* today?"
- "What orthopraxy is connected to the orthodoxy I am seeing here?"

# WRAPPING OUR HEADS AROUND IT

*(MISSIONAL ANALYSIS)*

## >>> 4

# LAODICEAN CUL-DE-SACS

### Western Affluence and Spiritual Bankruptcy

The house stirred my friends' memory, and he told how the old-time people used to visit each other in the evenings. There used to be a sort of institution in our part of the country known as "sitting till bedtime." After supper, when they weren't too tired, neighbors would walk across the fields to visit each other. They popped corn, my friend said, and ate apples and talked. Sometimes they told stories about each other, about themselves, living again in their own memories and thus keeping their memories alive. Among the hearers of these stories were always the children. When bedtime came, the visitors lit their lanterns and went home. My friend talked about this, and thought about it, and then he said, "They had everything but money."

Wendell Berry, *What Are People For?*

**T**he city that never sleeps."
"What happens there stays there."
"The Big Apple."

"The city by the bay."

First-century Laodicea was one of *those* cities, a happening place that seemed to have it all—style, money, and a bright future. In many ways it was an economic leader in the region. Laodicea was especially known as the world capital for a high-quality glossy black wool that well-to-do people from all over were especially fond of. It was also the spot where people from throughout the Roman Empire flocked in search of answers for many of their medical issues. It hosted the equivalent of today's Mayo Clinic. Home to one of the most well-known medical schools in the world, it was the place where a famous eye salve plus an ear ailment salve was developed. If television had been around then, surely infomercials would have blasted the airwaves with all that Laodicea had to offer.

Robust industry created an opportunity to capitalize exponentially on profits, and the wool and salve industry spawned a third industry that created even more wealth. Laodicea became a major hub for currency exchange and lending. It not only had a corner on the market in textiles and a world-famous medical industry, it was also a prosperous financial center. Historians of the time wrote much of the great wealth of Laodicea.

For such a hip city, Laodicea still had an embarrassing weakness. It lacked an adequate water source. Cold water had to be piped in from the abundant supply at Colossae, but this city was a good ten miles away, and by the time it arrived at Laodicea, it was lukewarm. Hot water was supplied from Hierapolis, home to natural hot springs, but this city was six miles away. So by the time the water arrived, it too was lukewarm. This was the backdrop for the following passage where Jesus speaks a stern warning to the church at Laodicea:

> To the angel of the church in Laodicea write: These are the words of the Amen, the faithful and true witness, the ruler of

God's creation. I know your deeds, that you are neither cold nor hot. I wish you were either one or the other! So, because you are lukewarm—neither hot nor cold—I am about to spit you out of my mouth. You say, "I am rich; I have acquired wealth and do not need a thing." But you do not realize that you are wretched, pitiful, poor, blind and naked. I counsel you to buy from me gold refined in the fire, so you can become rich; and white clothes to wear, so you can cover your shameful nakedness; and salve to put on your eyes, so you can see. (Rev. 3:14–18)

This is one of those smashmouth passages. Jesus turns his cap around backward and gets right in the face of the church of Laodicea. He lays into their pride and security by drawing a metaphor from something familiar to everyone there. Cold water quenches thirst and is a great refresher. Hot water has great medicinal value and is good for teas and soups. But what is lukewarm water good for? Nothing. It just hits the palate all wrong, and Jesus says that this is the true state of Laodicea. In spite of surface appearances, they are lukewarm, just like their water. The Laodiceans were no doubt self-conscious about their lack of hot water, so this message would have been like a direct hit in the solar plexus.

The Lord says their famous *black* wool fails to cover their own spiritual nakedness, the bankruptcy of their heart overshadows their material wealth, and the blindness of their spiritual eyes has left them in a directionless state. He admonishes them to seek clothing of *white*, a reference to purity of heart and righteousness. In essence Jesus says, "This eye salve you are making so much money on can't cure your own spiritual blindness. And your strong economy? It's really just a smoke screen for your spiritual bankruptcy."

Have you ever seen a football or rugby player who has really had his bell rung? He is on the bench, and the trainer places a vial of smelling salts under his nose. If the guy just sits there sniffing the ammonia, with no reaction, it's clear he's jacked up. A clearheaded person reacts immediately to smelling salts. Unless the player is totally out of it, his head snaps back and his eyes pop wide open. This is what the trainer hopes to see—the player shocked into awareness. This passage should do the same to us as Jesus followers in the current body of Christ in the West. The alarm here is that Jesus' accusations are not aimed at the secular city itself. We can't say, "Yeah, the *world* is screwed up." No, Jesus is not admonishing unbelievers in this passage. He is talking strictly to the *church* at Laodicea, not society at large.

The Laodicean church had become so comfortable and at one with the host culture that it left them with no noticeable difference in their way of life, concerns, and pursuits. The Christians there were manifesting the same proud, arrogant, and conceited attitude as the non-Christians. And they were pursuing the same agenda of prosperity, security, comfort, and convenience as the host culture.

Jesus' response is, "I want to spit you out of my mouth. You think everything is just fine and that you are on the right track . . . in need of *nothing*." Jesus points out that *nothing* can be done with people like this. He says, "I wish you were either hot or cold." Why would he say that?

A *cold* person is someone who is clearly far from God, is aware of it, and usually makes no bones about it. There is something I love about these people. Maybe it's their raw honesty. Brian is a friend of mine who would fall into the "cold" category. I deeply love and thoroughly enjoy being around him. We talk politics, spirituality, parenting, and sports—basic *life* stuff. The thing I appreciate about Brian is that he is up front with the fact that he has no interest in following Christ. He reads everything that Richard Dawkins writes and calls himself an *almost atheist*. He is extremely intelligent and has a smile that is contagious. I always tell him that when the light of God comes alive in him, he is going to be a Zorro for the kingdom of God. I actually have *hope* for Brian because he is cold regarding God. Imagine that.

The *hot* person is someone who is on fire for God. They are hungry for the things of the Lord and are available to him without hesitation. Christians like this have a fervent passion that blazes and spreads like wildfire. I call them *pyroGodiacs*.

But the lukewarm, *I'm-doin'-just-fine* Christian? There is nothing you can really do to get this person off center and growing in the Lord and participating in the kingdom agenda. No amount of honey, sugar, lemon, or stirring makes lukewarm taste better. The attitude of Jesus to this tenor of Christian must not be lost on us. The truth? Jesus can't stand these people—these . . . *Christians*. It is not so much that he is angry or grieved. He is just flat-out disgusted. Think about it. What happens when you take a swig of something that is lukewarm? Have you ever picked up a cup of coffee, expecting the hot, rich nectar of the Columbian bean to awake your senses, only to be startled by a lukewarm and "dead" flavor that just lies flat on your palate? If you are near a sink or outdoors, you likely spit it out. This is what Jesus is saying about the Laodicean church *and* all lukewarm Christians—"Yuck!"

**JUST SAYIN'...**

As I mentioned in the briefing chapter at the beginning of the book, to really make progress against the suffocating parts of popular culture, we must live with the mindset of a contrarian. We must recognize the entrapments of a consumerist culture and cultivate a life that resists its pull. This doesn't mean that we pull back from people. That is religious sectarianism and is actually the opposite of a truly missional stance. No, we live and demonstrate a better way of living— living from the kingdom paradigm. We must learn to live leaner and simpler. In a world that seeks to hold on to its "stuff" and even kill for it, we are the people who have learned to give it away—to be generous. In a world that demands "service," we position ourselves as servants, etc. In *Untamed* Deb and I call this "the great reversal," and it ought to be the lifestyle of a disciple.

—*Alan Hirsch*

## The American Dreamworld

It's hard not to see irony in the fact that the word *Laodicea* is a compound of two words: *laos* ("the peoples") and *dike* ("rights"). How fitting—"the people's rights"—as in the *right* to pursue happiness. A few years ago, in a sermon series on living missionally, I made the suggestion to members of our church to look for bargain clothing at thrift stores as a means of stewarding their money in more missional ways. My wife had been doing this with our family for some time, and it had become a bit of a treasure hunt for us. This suggestion took on tremendous momentum, and a group of our folks even printed and made copies of a booklet that mapped out and gave descriptions of secondhand clothing stores in the St. Louis area. We even had quick fashion shows on Sunday mornings where people would wear their "new" outfits and share the price they paid. It became a common sight to see someone in our foyer twirl and tug on her clothes, saying, "Salvation Army Store, Brentwood. Two bucks!"

The Laodicean spirit didn't take this lying down. One person in our church took great offense that I would make such a suggestion and "shove it down people's throats." "He has no place telling me how to spend *my* money. I have the right to spend *my* money the way *I* want," was the response. As the thrift store movement trudged on, it wasn't long until this family felt "led" to move to another church. I felt like Jerry Maguire, defending his vision statement. "It was just a *suggestion!*" I said.

I think it is fair to say that for most Christians in the West, the dominant forces that shape their lives run counter to the values of Jesus. Like weekend tourists, the Christian majority is obliviously floating downstream, soaking in the same concerns, wants, and agendas of the prevailing culture, drifting wherever the current takes them. Oh, we still have the common headline-grabbing moral values and issues that typically arise during political election seasons. "Values" bumper stickers are pasted all over the rafts and inner tubes of the Christian party as it floats in the same direction as those it points fingers at.

What has happened to our values when it comes to the vices of covetousness, the unbridled consumption of earthly goods, gluttony, and the amassing of more and more with no end in sight? Most of this happens with little or no regard for the needs or plight of those whose backs Western consumption is built upon, much less the destruction it's doing to our own lives and God-given calling. This has contributed to a lukewarm Christianity that is the norm in the so-called evangelical world. Pope John Paul II said it well:

> Before our eyes we have the results of ideologies such as Marxism, Nazism and Fascism, and also of myths like racial superiority, nationalism and ethnic exclusivism. No less pernicious, though not always as obvious, are the effects of materialistic consumerism, in which the exaltation of the individual and the selfish satisfaction of personal aspirations become the ultimate goal of life. In this outlook, the negative effects on others are considered completely irrelevant.[1]

The pursuit of happiness has left a trail of tears on many fronts. Convenient online banking, trendy fashion, iPods, and high-def televisions are not giving us more to smile about. In fact, depression and mental illness have increased in direct proportion to our wealth index. Though the United States has the highest standard of living on the planet, it has been over fifty years since Americans described themselves to pollsters as "very happy."[2] Bigger and better has not equated to happy and happier.

The average American home is now more than double the size of a home from the 1950s. The irony here is that the average American family is smaller now than it was in the '50s. Though families are smaller, the definition of "necessities" grows almost yearly. What we think we *need* to survive ranges from mobile phones to air-conditioning, to at least two

127

cars. America is an *I-want-my-own-I-want-it-now-I-want-it-big-and-I-want-it-the way-I-want-it* culture. And the average American Christian is just as drunk on consumerism as the non-Christian at the other end of the bar. *American Mania* author Peter Whybrow says:

> A variety of surveys conducted during the 1980s and 1990s recorded a declining satisfaction with life in America. Why, for example, does nearly one-third of the U.S. population now struggle with the complications of obesity? And why, amid our drive for wealth and self-improvement, are the best-selling drugs on the American market those prescribed for the stress-related diseases of ulcer, depression, and high blood pressure? In our demand-driven, debt-saturated culture many families find themselves too pressured to enjoy, even to notice, their affluence. Time is chronically in short supply and the "free moments" that once balanced a busy life have all but disappeared. The demands of securing and maintaining material wealth in a rapidly shifting economic climate—particularly for Americans who shoulder considerable debt—have created an accelerated, competitive lifestyle that steals away sleep and kindles anxiety, threatening the intimate social webs that sustain family and community.[3]

Fallen human nature defaults to self-preservation, lust, greed, and longing for power. Just place three Oreos in a room of four five-year-olds and watch nature take its course. Somebody's *gonna* be crying real soon. On the other hand, self-restraint, mercy, empathy for others, and giving are learned behavior. The church is God's ideal social order and there is to be a significant, life-altering economic side of the kingdom of God that comes to bear on all who seek to follow Jesus as Lord. In *Faith and Wealth*, Justo González remarks, "Themes of economic justice appear repeatedly in the preaching of Jesus and of the early movement. They show up often in the background, as in the many parables that deal with economic matters, (such as) the laborers in the vineyard, the unjust steward, the talents, and so forth. And they appear in the foreground, often in starker terms and with more radical demands."[4]

This mindset is all but lost in Western Christianity. On any given weekend, churches are filled with Christians sitting shoulder to shoulder. Some have the financial wherewithal to drive expensive cars that they take to the car wash each week. Others can't afford to have the brakes repaired on the fifteen-year-old rust bucket they drive to a minimum-wage job. In the same church "family," many Christians leave for weekends on the lake while others lay awake on Friday nights, worrying over what their children will eat for the next two days because a free school lunch won't be available.

 **JUST SAYIN'. . .**

The heart of discipleship is unfettered adherence to Christ, his message, and his values. He makes absolute claim to our loyalty and allegiance. When we become entangled in addictive consumption, we are complicit in many of the unjust ways and means of production of the very commodities we absorb. Jesus disturbed the status quo and rallied against injustice and lack of mercy. He was both an advocate and an answer for the marginalized and oppressed. If Jesus, the great deliverer, lives in us, how can we be anything but charged with the same concern and vigor?

— *Alan Hirsch*

For too long, church culture has steamed down the channel of self-centeredness and away from community building and societal transformation. We need a radical reformation of leadership that preaches, models, and leads with a message that stirs us away from the trending ascendance of personal ambition.

When cultures get out of kilter and lose balance, extremes start to dominate and gain momentum. Laodicean culture in the church has done this very thing. As American wealth and appetite for more and more increased over the last three decades, social inequality did as well. The gap between the wealthiest Americans and everyone else is currently greater than in any industrialized nation. At a human level the implications have been devastating. The purchasing power for the bottom quarter of the population actually decreased by 50 percent in the last twenty-five years of the twentieth century.

At the other end of the stick is the income of the average chief executive of a large American company, whose salary "rose approximately 500 percent, from $1.8 million to $10.6 million per annum. This income is 419 times the earnings of a typical production worker."[5] In fact, if minimum wage maintained pace with the rate increase of CEO pay scales over the last twenty years, a worker earning minimum wage would receive over $23 per hour.

The economic downfall at the close of the first decade of the new millennium threw the financial brakes on for just about all of America and the entire industrialized world. The church must have—in the words of Jesus—"ears to hear" if we have a true desire to make a right here, right now missional impact.

## Misplaced Desire and Imagination Lost

It wasn't so long ago that clothing labels were on the *inside* of our clothing. Today, not just teenagers but middle-aged adults as well are more than happy to spend $24.95 for a T-shirt with *Aeropostale* or *Abercrombie & Fitch* emblazoned across the front. Now, in the spirit of honesty, I'll tell one on myself. Seconds after I wrote that last sentence, I looked down and saw that I was wearing an *American Eagle* T-shirt. Thankfully, I can also say that this shirt came from a thrift store. I paid two bucks for it. What is wrong with us, though? What a racket we have bought into! Before we exit *Joe's Crab Shack* or *Cheesecake Factory*, we fork over good money for a sweatshirt, paying *them* for the privilege of becoming a human billboard. Why do we not consider this to be insanity? We have been branded on the inside . . . made to think that we can overcome loneliness and alienation by being part of a brand identity and community! Who's defining us now?

A mid-1990's advertising campaign for Canon cameras featured tennis star Andre Agassi with the tagline "Image is everything." Early capitalism has been rightly viewed as a shift from "being to having"; modern capitalist culture has gone from "having to appearing." Guy Debord summed this up in his book *The Society of the Spectacle.* Debord's argument was that commodities have taken over the imagination of society and the spectacle itself became the commodity. The need to be noticed and accepted by others has trumped needs for basics.

The critical issue for us as Christians is that consumerism seeks to shape and dictate our identity. In the process our true personhood as strangers and aliens of God's kingdom is snuffed out. In terms of risk, time, finance, and energy, we can't afford to *be* missional. We can't even conceive of such a life. The apostle John warned against this very thing:

> Don't love the world's ways. Don't love the world's goods. Love of the world squeezes out love for the Father. Practically everything that goes on in the world—wanting your own way, wanting everything for yourself, wanting to appear important—has nothing to do with the Father. It just isolates you from him. The world and all its wanting, wanting, wanting is on the way out—but whoever does what God wants is set for eternity. (1 John 2:15–17 Message)

Each Christmas season is met with sermons, magazine articles, and internet blogs that decry the commercialization of Christmas. Pastors preach sermons that voice disdain over Jesus' birth being obscured by the orgy of shopping, warning followers not to take the bait. I really don't know what all the fuss is about. Christmastime is simply a grand finale to a year's worth of consumption. It should be no surprise

131

## JUST SAYIN'...

When at all costs we hold the nuclear family and middle-class concepts at the pinnacle of our priorities, we become dull and blind to the injustices around us. Family ideals and the American Dream hold loyalty over and above the initiative of the kingdom of God and the justice and mercy it calls for. The presumptive "If you believe it, you can become it" notion causes many in the middle class to dismiss their obligation to those who are homeless or to interpret the plight of the poor as reaping a harvest from their own lazy lack of initiative. That is, at least, until the middle class themselves become unemployed as has occurred in the recent economic crash—then it's someone else's fault.

—*Alan Hirsch*

that his birth is overshadowed— for the whole year leading up to Christmas, the *life* of Jesus is suppressed by consumption in the lives of his followers.

The verse above speaks to the danger of loving consumer goods and the fact that this misplaced desire suffocates love for God and the things he would have us desire. Jesus urges us to lay up treasures in the heavens (Matt. 6:20) rather than invest in earthly treasure. In the parable of the sower, Jesus speaks of how the love for other things chokes God's Word from taking root in our hearts (Matt. 13:1–9).

The plethora of New Testament Scripture that speaks of loving one another, sharing with others, and substantially caring for the poor make little headway into the imagination of most American Christians. These passages are simply not taken seriously. "I can't open my home up to that lady and her two toddlers. I know she has no place to live and I have a spare bedroom, but that's just not *practical* for me at this time in my life." Individualism and our desire for comfort and privacy choke out the Word and our missional imagination along with it, nullifying our effectiveness as agents of the kingdom of God. Vincent Miller wrote about the shutting down of our imagination due to our fixation with the American Dream:

Two generations ago, it was not uncommon for families to raise five or more children in small, two- or three-room houses. Our inability today to imagine how this was possible is a testament to the psychological skills we have lost. Now it is a common expectation that each child should have her or his own room. This social arrangement requires an enormous amount of resources and renders us less able to share our dwellings with others in hospitality. Social isolation and the burdens of maintaining a family in this system make it unlikely that other people's needs will ever present themselves. If and when we do encounter them, we are likely to be so preoccupied with the tasks of maintaining our immediate families that we will have little time and resources to offer. The geography of the single-family home makes it very likely that we will care more about the feeding of our pets than about the millions of children who go to bed hungry around us.[6]

We need to recover the vision of ourselves as being made in the image of God and to shine with that image. Agassi was right; image *is* everything. We just must make sure we have the *right* image in mind.

Speaking of the enormous potential for being ensnared by desire for money and riches, social action author Ronald Sider says, "Possessions are positively dangerous because they often encourage unconcern for the poor . . . and because they seduce people into forsaking God. Even more, they put people in the never ending loop of covetousness."[7]

There is an old saying that goes, "How much does it take to make a man happy? Answer: Just a little bit more." Consumerism trains our eyes downward to the base things of the earth. It keeps us from pursuing the things from above. The real spiritual danger here is not so much in the rightful use of a particular item but rather in the *pursuit* of the item. It is when we are being defined and shaped by what we consume—it's called *conspicuous consumption*, and the marketers are quite deliberate in trying to shape our identity and self-worth and relate it to the product. Marketers understand this better than

## JUST SAYIN'...

All factors point to signs that Christianity is in decline in the West. We must own the fact that the way we live out our faith is culpable, at least in large part. A domesticated, tamed version of Christianity that is mired in the same wants, desires, and traps of the watching world yields no appeal. Missional movements flourish because a group of people have been changed by Jesus, and the change is made abundantly clear through living in an alternative Jesus-like society of love, grace, and generosity. For most of us, this means we must simply begin to step out beyond our self-imposed barriers of safety and security and risk, joining the Holy Spirit in what God is doing in our neighborhoods and cities.

—*Alan Hirsch*

we do and feed the bottomless stomach of consumers with more and more items to consume. The objects of desire come faster and faster. Miller says, "The bitterness of disappointment and frustration with particular objects of desire is endlessly glazed over by the sweetness of desire for new ones."[8]

## Domesticated Risk

Inherent within the roots of Christianity is a steely, risk-it-all resolve. But the prevailing forms of American Christianity seem to know little of such notions. Individualism, consumption, and the pursuit of the American Dream have effectively sedated most Christians, lulling them into a passive, risk-averse state of comfort, safety, and security. This is a drug that has numbed us to the pain and needs around us, needs that we often have the means to heal and meet. The very idea that living generously and courageously should be normative for Christians just sounds like crazy talk. It's not "practical."

For most Christians, a "good Christian life" means my children believe in Jesus and actually enjoy going to church, my wife and I give 10 percent of our income to the church, we keep our car radio tuned to the Christian radio station (which, incidentally, proclaims itself as "safe for the whole family"), and we watch movies that have lots of cursing but we never use those words ourselves . . . out loud at least.

We can choose to either batten down the hatches and live a bunkered life of preserving what we have, just *surviving* the evils of this world. Or, we can choose to embrace our newborn identity as aliens in a strange land and pick up the mantle of living redemptively. The second choice means we embrace, rather than resist, the mindset of the Great Redeemer—Jesus Christ. It means we hold on loosely to the temporal things of the earth and we live as available agents of the kingdom of God. We will look at some ways we can do so in the next chapter.

## IDEAS AND SUGGESTIONS FOR FORMING A MISSIONAL LIFESTYLE

*Examine your heart*

- Honestly ask yourself:
  - » Do labels and brand names matter to me?
  - » Is my imagination held captive to commodities and hollow images?

*Discover and act*

- Find out if there are others in your church family in need. Can you do something about it? Do you have the means to help?

*Open up*

- Do you have a spare bedroom in your home? Could your children share a bedroom or can you convert your garage into a spare room for someone who needs a place to stay? If so, offer the room for free or affordably to someone in need.

# >>> 5

# LOSING FOR WINNING

*Freeing Ourselves to Live Missionally*

The only ones among you who will be truly happy are
those who will have sought and found how to serve.

Albert Schweitzer

Therefore, since we have so great a cloud of witnesses
surrounding us, let us also lay aside every encumbrance
and the sin which so easily entangles us, and let us run
with endurance the race that is set before us.

Hebrews 12:1 NASB

There are times that *losing* can lead to winning, and
anyone who is serious about living missionally has to
do just that. Like any athletic competition, to run the
missional race means one must be in shape, and this almost
always requires shedding extra weight. When a person is out
of shape, it is difficult to breathe and oftentimes the heart

struggles to work properly. The same is true when we are spiritually fat. It is hard to draw in the breath and inspiration of God, and our hearts become hardened to the economy of his kingdom. In this chapter we want to consider what some of that weight might be, along with ways we can lose it and get in missional shape.

Each season the television show *The Biggest Loser* begins with the contestants attempting a one-mile run. All of the participants are dangerously overweight and this task is monumental for each one. It seems impossible. There have been times when contestants collapsed and were taken to the hospital. At the conclusion of the season, the remaining contestants run a full marathon. Three months previously, many of them could barely complete a one-mile run and now they are able to run over twenty-six miles. They can now do something way beyond their wildest dreams because they have shed weight and adopted a healthy lifestyle.

Most Americans have developed lives of excess to the point that we cannot even dream of doing some of the things we would really love to do for others because our lives are just too fat and bogged down with excess in so many ways. To engage in living missionally means we must get our lives into missional shape. A lot of people would love to be able to run a marathon, but they love eating Twinkies more. By the same token, most Christians would love to make an impact in their communities, but they have not shaped their lives to be able to keep pace.

By mere observation it seems clear to me that, along with Easter lilies and chirping birds, a sign that spring has sprung each year is the American institution known as the garage sale. Most North American families have enough stuff to conduct one of these events every two or three years. If you have ever been foolhardy enough to hold your own garage (or yard) sale, you know that people start knocking on your door the evening before or early the morning of your sale in order to get first shot at acquiring your stuff. We love stuff. We love getting it, we love having it, and we love to search for more. And we have so much that we have to shed some of it every few seasons to make room for more.

Another icon of consumption is the self-storage building. I have a personal conspiracy theory. I am convinced that there is collusion between exercise equipment manufacturers and the storage building industry. I think they are one and the same and they're making money on both ends. They sell us equipment they know we won't use and then rent us a place to store it. Brilliant! Scattered throughout our cities and suburbs are large self-storage properties occupying prime real estate. For several years now I have brought this up in sermons as a passing observation, but I was blown away by the data as I began to take a closer look into the facts.

**JUST SAYIN'. . .**

The hidden danger of unbridled consumption is that in the end we are the ones being consumed. Our freedom for true joy and our ability to live out our God-given calling as agents of the King is swallowed up and entangled in the web of consumption. But when we are freed from the love and greedy acquisition of more things, we are liberated to be generous transmitters of Jesus' phenomenal grace and kindness. This yields a real and lasting fulfillment that leaves the consumerist pursuit of happiness in the dust.

—*Alan Hirsch*

Labeled by some as *catacombs of consumption*, there are currently over 52,000 self-storage locations in the United States with revenue of over 23 billion dollars. With the fastest rate of growth in commercial real estate, it is an industry more profitable than Hollywood. One in ten American families rents self-storage units. Storage units have become the "spare tire" around the waistline of American consumption. Just imagine the needs that could be met with the disbursement of our stored stuff and the money saved on storage rental if we would abandon our addiction to stuff and adapt the practices of God's kingdom economics. Our ability to touch the lives of others would expand greatly. Fewer goods would mean more goodness.

Jesus was continually warning his followers of the dangers of hoarding up for oneself:

> Then He said to them, "Beware, and be on your guard against every form of greed; for not even when one has an abundance does his life consist of his possessions." And He told them a parable, saying, "The land of a rich man was very productive. And he began reasoning to himself, saying, 'What shall I do, since I have no place to store my crops?' Then he said, 'This is what I will do: I will tear down my barns and build larger ones, and there I will store all my grain and my goods. And I will say to my soul, "Soul, you have many goods laid up for many years to come; take your ease, eat, drink and be merry."' But God said to him, 'You fool! This very night your soul is required of you; and now who will own what you have prepared?' So is the man who stores up treasure for himself, and is not rich toward God." (Luke 12:15–21 NASB)

This parable is a great description of the malady of Western consumption and greed. And it is critical that we call it what it is. We must begin by judging whether we are really serious about positioning ourselves to participate missionally right here and right now. The first step in breaking an addiction is to call it what it is and to admit our participation in it. The sky doesn't fall when we admit our sin and failures. It actually opens up and the clouds begin to break apart. When God brings correction and rebuke into our lives, it is not so that he can blow off steam. He chastises us out of his love and desire to get us on track to drawing our life out of the well of himself.

### Be Unconformed to Be Transformed

In Luke 16:13 Jesus says, "No servant can serve two masters; for either he will hate the one and love the other, or else he will be devoted to one and despise the other. You cannot serve God and wealth" (NASB). Just a few verses following this one, Jesus tells a parable about a rich man who ignored a poor beggar living on his front porch. When people become obsessed with gain, they unwittingly become servants of wealth while stepping over the poor as they pursue happiness for themselves.

Most of us are under the illusion that we don't have enough resources to help others. For most Americans this is just not true. We've become blinded to the resources we have that are tied up in a lifestyle our culture has carved out for us. Satan works within cultural systems and structures to capture our will through our *wants*. We then begin to chase our wants at the expense of our God-given call and ability to discern his will for our lives. The apostle Paul warned of this: "And do not be conformed to this world, but be

**JUST SAYIN'...**

True missional Christianity both reclaims and redeems culture. It is no good just railing against the sins of greed and materialism; our task is not just to expose idolatry for what it is but also to point people to the true Source of meaning. The freedom we experience by joining our hearts to the King of all also sets us free from devotion to the idols of materialism. We are set free in our hearts and minds to the liberating awareness that we do not have to waste our lives on meaningless things. When we do this, we will be the good news to a world captive to the consumerist lusts, beauty myths, peer acceptance, etc., that drive so many of us to live lives that are less than God intended.

—*Alan Hirsch*

transformed by the renewing of your mind, so that you may prove what the will of God is, that which is good and acceptable and perfect" (Rom. 12:2 NASB).

This verse points out that when we allow ourselves to be shaped and overly influenced by the host culture, not only are our minds not transformed by the thoughts of God, but we find it difficult if not impossible to discern his will for our lives. It has become hard for most Christians in the West to dream missionally, much less discern God's marching orders for their lives because they are so tied to the kingdom of the present age that their minds are numb to his Word. As Vincent Miller says, "The abstraction inherent in consumer desire absorbs not only our own ability to determine how much is enough but also our ability to engage the needs of *others.*"[1]

The good news . . . no . . . the great news is that we don't have to continue this way. We can "unconform" and position ourselves to live missionally right now.

## Think "Redeem"

Anyone who has seen the movie *Schindler's List* will remember the touching scene near the end of the movie. Leaving the factory where he has spent his fortune bribing the German SS in order to secure the lives of Jewish workers, Oskar Schindler breaks down as he looks upon the faces of the people he has saved (over 1,100 people) and then upon the car he is about to enter. He begins to weep, and mumbles, "This car . . . ten more people." He staggers and clutches at the gold lapel pen on his blazer. "This pen . . . two more people." He cries, "I could have done more. I could have done more . . ." Schindler had developed a mindset of redemption. His situation was rare in that there was an actual trade-off of people's lives for possessions. He could literally redeem people's lives in exchange for money or valuables.

Most of us will never face such a situation to the extent that Oskar Schindler did, but every day we do have a choice of how to spend our lives, our possessions, and our finances. We can bring redemption to people's lives if we steward our resources in that direction. Our lives are full of choices that determine our ability to participate in mission and mission's purpose—redemption. Our heavenly Father is a restoring

God. He is the mender of hearts and the advocate of the least and the lost, and Jesus' agenda was all about this very thing. Scripture instructs us to have the same mindset as Jesus (Phil. 2:5). So, if we are true to our born-again nature, we will seek ways to redeem broken people and situations that are within our power or influence.

Throughout the Bible we see the redemptive nature of God. Just observe his hand upon Abraham's offspring, specifically the nation of Israel, which was to be a light to the Gentiles (Isa. 49:6). As history progressed, God's redemptive plan unfolded. Following the death and resurrection of Jesus, the church was born and the next phase of redemption was revealed. Access to God would no longer be through a single nation or temple. God had now moved into a spiritual temple, his redeemed people from all nations. This is where we—the church—come in.

Redemption itself is in us, and we not only have the opportunity, but also the obligation, to spread it wherever we go. It is not relegated to our church buildings, systems, or clergy members. It is in every single one of us, right here, right now. Redemption needs no organization or ordination. It simply needs a host. It can be dispersed and released through the life of any Christ follower. As redemption-minded people, we will look at those around us, from the workplace to the grocery store, as those we hope to spread the peace of God upon. Ronald Sider, Philip Olson, and Heidi Unruh point to Jeremiah's letter to the captive exiles of Israel:

> Jeremiah passed on the Lord's instructions to the exiles: "Build houses and live in them; plant gardens and eat what they produce. Take wives and have sons and daughters" (Jer. 29:5–6). The exiled Israelites were to provide for basic necessities such as food and housing and to rebuild their shattered family lives. Then God called them to go a step farther: "Seek the welfare of the city where I have sent you into exile, and pray to the Lord on its behalf, for in its welfare you will find your welfare" (v. 7). As the Israelites worked to meet personal

and family needs, they were also to seek the good of their new home city. God's plan for the Israelites rested not just on their personal well-being but on their becoming a positive influence on the wider society.[2]

## Rich toward God

To start with, we must decide we *are* going to do this. We must make our minds up that we will disentangle ourselves from the suffocating weight that comes with living an overly consumptive lifestyle. We make a *choice* to break free in order to live redemptively. This requires an honest evaluation of the differences between our *needs* and *wants* and how we use what we have for redemptive purposes. We must decide whether we would prefer to gather treasures for earthly living or invest in heavenly treasure, being rich toward God. And a hint for where to lay up heavenly treasure is to recognize that the only things that will last forever are not even things; they are *people.* So if we desire to lay up treasures in heaven, we need to look to how we can affect the lives of others.

My wife and I are continually amazed as we watch television shows that track people's searches for a new house. Time and time again the pursuit of a larger house comes about as couples discover they have a first or second child on the way. In many cases the house they live in is quite large, but the default mode is, "We have a child on the way . . . we need more space." It's as if the pregnancy test included drinking some wacked-out "you need more space" Kool-aid.

Over the last half-century, Americans have been conditioned to believe that they need larger and larger houses. The first Levittown subdivision homes following World War II contained 750 square feet. "By the '60s 1,100 square feet was typical, and by the '70s, 1,350. Now it's 2,469."[3] Compare this to the average home size in the United Kingdom, which is just over 750 square feet. For *some* reason we have come to believe we must have more and more personal space. My best guess is that the desire for independence and privacy drives this.

When purchasing a home or a vehicle, the tendency is to make choices based on the maximum amount of money we can obtain through credit. This is what we deem "affordable." Structuring our lives in this way means we are left with little to nothing with which to live missionally and respond to spontaneous needs we happen upon. If living as an ambassador for the kingdom of God is really more important to us than the largest house or nicest car we can "afford," we will make purchasing decisions based on this criteria rather than on credit limits. We will base purchasing decisions on *missional* limits. We will look at our living expenses and ask what we can afford in order to live missionally. We add missional living to our budget and take it into consideration as we make major purchases or significant lifestyle decisions. For just about everyone, the largest financial investment we have is our home. It is usually our most valuable asset and therefore we should consider how to use it for kingdom means.

**JUST SAYIN'...**

God is the Creator. One of the exciting things is that we are being like God when we are creative, and one of the ways in which we are creative is to use our imaginations. The fundamental job of the sanctified imagination is to create from the society we live in a vision for the society we want to live in. As Bono has said, "Dream up the world you want to live in, dream out loud, at high volume!"

—*Alan Hirsch*

## Many Ways, but One Purpose

As we consider what living this way means for our families and us personally, it is important to keep in mind that the Spirit of God works in a wide variety of ways. It is easy to draw on situations and stories we see in the Bible and assume they are commandments. This is the classic *descriptive* versus *prescriptive* mistake. There are many situations in Scripture

145

that explain "what" happened without God telling us to do the same. Jesus once used spit to make a dab of mud and put it on a blind man's eye, restoring his sight. But Jesus didn't tell us to "go and do likewise." God leads his people in many diverse ways and as we consider how to use the stuff we have for the purposes of God, we need to recognize this in our own lives as well as the lives of others.

It just may be that God wants you to have a large house with several bedrooms in order to be able to respond to folks who are without a home and need help getting back on their feet. I've known several families, including my own parents, who opened their homes up to people who needed a roof over their heads for a period of time. When they moved to the US, Alan and Deb were welcomed into the home of some dear friends who are empty nesters, where they lived for two years. Mike and Rita have made a significant investment in Alan and Deb's ministry and are partners in their fruit. Making a choice for housing, when viewed from the perspective of missional Christianity, will mean a commitment to live in the overflow of the good news of the kingdom of God. Western Seminary professor James Brownson points out the many ways the Holy Spirit inspires us to live "kingdomly":

> In living out its life under the cross, the early church found a variety of ways to say "no" to human assumptions and values. Some early Christians lived lives of radical voluntary poverty. A good example is found in Jesus' commission to his own disciples before their preaching tour in Matthew 10:5–10 and Luke 10:1–2. Here they are to take no money, not even a spare set of clothes. They are to be living examples of a radical trust in God, a kind of trust that shatters our ordinary assumptions about what we need to get by. They are to be a living sign that shakes the world loose from its anxious reliance on possessions. In this sense, they are a precursor to the cross itself. But notice something. Who takes care of these itinerant poor preachers? It was believers who had homes, families, and food to spare! Without them, the preaching missions would

have been impossible. Hence, this call to radical poverty is not a call to the whole church; it is a call to *some* in the church as an expression of the cross. Likewise Paul calls some to celibacy in 1 Corinthians 7:32–35. These are a sign to the world that sex is not the be-all and end-all of life. But again, this call is not for everyone. The Christians in Acts 4 pooled their possessions as a radical challenge to the world's tendency to horde [sic] and isolate. But again, there is no evidence that this pattern was normative in early Christianity.[4]

Brownson's description celebrates the creativity of God in the lives of Christ followers who are open and obedient to his ways and means in their lives. We need both a radically lean way of living by some disciples and an elaborate abundance shared by others. Brownson lists several authentic *needs* for a kingdom economy to manifest:

- We need people who are called to a radical simplicity of lifestyle, to remind the rest of us that we don't need what we think we need.
- We need people committed to celibacy, to tell us that sex is neither a necessity nor a god.
- We need people who are lavish in prayer and spiritual disciplines, in order to remind those of us with harder spirits of where our real help comes from.
- We need communities of Christians willing to commit themselves to support each other in risky, venturesome ways, to goad the rest of us out of our autonomy.
- We need Christians willing to resist the many ways in which the dominant in our world crush the weak.
- We need Christians who find a thousand joyful ways to take the screwed-up values of this world and turn them upside down.[5]

One of the hallmarks of the recent economic recession in the United States, the worst situation since the Great Depression, has been the loss of homes through foreclosure and the inability to pay rent. The housing market has made it very difficult to sell a house for those who would like to downsize. But what if we were to look at the current situation as an opportunity to flex our missional muscles? You may not be able to move into a home that is less expensive, but you very well may have extra space or you might be able to make extra space by having your children share a bedroom.

Austin and Brian Chu are two brothers who recently traveled across the United States filming a documentary about the current recession titled *The Recess Ends*. They traveled in a small van and relied on the generosity of friends and strangers for lodging. One family who provided food and shelter was the Frankels, of Albuquerque, New Mexico. Chris and Georgia Frankel were once in a situation where they had to rely on friends and family to get by but are now in a more solid financial position and are living their lives in a pay-it-forward mode. In addition to their own three children, the couple shares their home with five adults and two teenagers.

> But even with a lifestyle Chris describes as "living paycheck to paycheck," the couple say they are fortunate to have a large house (it's more than 3,800 square feet) that has become a haven for those living there. "People were there for us and helped us when we needed it," Chris said. "We wanted to do the same." . . . The couple has converted spare rooms into bedrooms to accommodate everyone, and even with a food bill that averages about $1,000 a month, Georgia swears she wouldn't have it any other way. "I feel like everyone needs a good environment to live in," Georgia said. "We have a home we were blessed with, and it has a lot of room for everybody. We work well as a family." . . . "My kids get to experience different cultures and different kinds of people," [Chris] said. "At the end of the day, if it comes down between saving a dollar or helping someone else out, we have been pretty good about seeing the investment in our friendships and our family. That's what keeps us going and keeps us pretty happy."[6]

## Baggage of Status and Power

When Satan was tempting Jesus in the desert, he not only offered possessions, he also offered power and status. His m.o. to gain control over the hearts of God's people has not changed. Satan uses economic power and status to steer the hearts and minds of the upper class and powerlessness and lack to defeat and oppress the lower classes. But Jesus engenders meekness in his followers, leaving them unanchored to the weights of worldly status and reputation.

It is impossible to know what is in our own hearts until we are tested. Like addicts in denial, there are a lot of things in our lives that we believe we can let go of; things that we think we are in control of when in fact they are in control of us. Several years ago Sherri began to wean our family off the addiction of name-brand clothing. In fact, she took it a step further and started weaning us off the "must-have" of *new* clothing when she started retraining us to begin any shopping search at the used clothing stores. I was both surprised and disappointed in myself as my inner attitudes began to surface.

## JUST SAYIN'...

I really believe that idolatry is the category of sin that describes the brokenness pervading contemporary society and paradoxically is also the key that will unlock the hearts of people in the West. In short, idolatry is any attempt to establish meaning and purpose on our own terms and outside of a relationship with God—or as theologian Paul Tillich defined it, giving ultimate value to that which is not ultimate. This false grab for meaning goes on every day in our marketplaces, businesses, and domestic lives. Not all of us feel "guilty before God," but all will readily admit that we are ensnared by false gods of greed, lust, relationships, and the like. Because of the total pervasiveness of the media and the market, idolatry in all its forms presents a far more insidious challenge to the claims of Jesus over our lives because, in so many ways, it impacts each and every one of us, every day.

—*Alan Hirsch*

149

**JUST SAYIN'...**

Lance has described the result of "status anxiety." Endemic to modern society, it comes from any one or more of the following sources: (i) our anxious need for love and acceptance amidst a world of loneliness and lovelenessess; (ii) high expectations of ourselves, of what media and advertising suggest that life should offer, and from our peers; (iii) living in a meritocracy—the cultural and social system based on ability, talent, and competence; and (iv) having our social agenda being set by snobs—those who adopt the view that some people are inherently inferior to them for any one of a variety of reasons, and are generally impossible to please. Any—or a combination—of these can create status anxiety, which in turn creates a very distinct form of unhappiness. For instance, observe how you feel when a neighbor gets a new car, acquires a coveted piece of fashion, or remodels the kitchen.

—*Alan Hirsch*

If I had had those cartoon balloons hovering above my head, revealing my thoughts as we shopped, it would have been humiliating. I would think to myself, "I wish there was a way to let these people know I don't *have* to shop here . . . that I am doing this as a choice." This is love of status—the sin of pride. In the beginning I was very uncomfortable. I wanted to come out of Macy's toting a designer bag with the twisted paper handle as we strolled toward Gloria Jean's to pick up a caramel non-fat latte. I didn't want to walk out of Rudy's Last Chance Threads, with my jeans in a leftover plastic Wal-Mart bag. It didn't matter that the jeans were in perfect shape and cost less than the latte would have.

Before this experience, I had no clue that such attitudes were in my heart. Today I can honestly say that I have never cared less about the status of clothing brands than I do now. Sure, I enjoy nice clothes, but they are low on the priority list. I would much rather find and wear good clothing that is recycled or purchased at one of the closeout places such as Ross or T. J. Maxx. This is just good stewardship and leaves more money in my pocket to do better things with it.

I've often thought that Jesus could have entered Jerusalem on a large white stallion. Instead, the humble carpenter chose a baby donkey for his triumphal entry. This is like choosing an old Chevy over a Maserati. For some, cars just may be a bigger status symbol than houses. Other than a house, the most expensive purchase for the average person is an automobile. They are also the most depreciating purchases we make. New cars lose around 30 percent in value after leaving the car lot. A person can save multiple thousands of dollars over the years by making wise purchases of used cars. Insurance rates on used cars are substantially cheaper and services like Carfax along with a thorough mechanical inspection can go a long way toward making a smart buy.

## Kingdom Economics

God has revealed to us the way a society should live. A study of the book of Deuteronomy paints a picture of a culture with lifestyle habits that make for a sustainable and workable life. One of the things I love about this picture is not only a generous and caring society for one's fellow man but also the idea of the Sabbath and the feasts. God is no prude. He demands we work for a living, but for reasons of social justice and spirituality, he also demands that we rest. He demands we share and live selflessly, but he also requires that we always take extended breaks and throw parties.

A few years ago I decided to lose some extra weight. Untucked shirts hid the flab above my belt, but I knew it was there and that it was unhealthy. I also knew "dieting" was not the answer. Diets are only temporary fixes and almost always leave the person reverting to old habits and the previous form. I chose a program that would carve out a healthy lifestyle of eating right, good foods, combined with good exercise. One of the things I loved about the disciplines in the system I chose was that it provides for a "free" day—a type of a Sabbath from the "work" of living healthy. This means that one day a week I can eat anything I choose. If I want bacon and hash browns for breakfast, coconut pie at lunch, followed by dinner at my favorite Tex-Mex restaurant, then I can go for it.

The first week I was on the program, I couldn't wait until my free day. I went straight to Whataburger (the best hamburger in the world, none of that nonsense about In-N-Out Burger—this is something Alan and I both agree strongly on and it is a closed discussion) and guess what? I couldn't finish the meal. After six days my body had already begun to change and wanted less of what was really not good for me in excess. As I moved forward this dynamic continued, and my desires and "tastes" began to change. From that point on I didn't live for the *free* day. But when I was with friends or family on a special occasion, I was able to feast and enjoy with no guilt.

The same thing happens when we develop a lifestyle of living missionally. We can still enjoy the fruit of our labor, but we develop new appetites that are in check, not out of control. God carves out an economic design for our lives that is full of life for others *and* ourselves. In *How to Inherit the Earth*, Scott Bessenecker says:

> Those who are meek and who are submitted to the government of God will seek for his kingdom to come before all else, because they treasure this kingdom more than they treasure personal wealth. They are attentive to those who are weak and who are trampled underfoot by the powerful. They turn into great centrifuges of wealth, spinning their possessions out to those in need and stretching their arms out to those on the margins of society. This isn't trickle-down economics where a few at the top might slop some of what they have accumulated over the edge so that a drop or two trickles down to the masses at the bottom. Kingdom economics is pictured in the poor widow who was so insanely generous that she gave away the little she had to live on (Mark 12:41–44). In

kingdom economics the followers of Jesus pool their resources and then dole them out to each one as they have need (Acts 4:32–34). Widows and orphans are cared for in their distress (James 1:27). Homes are open for the homeless and clothing is given away to those who need it (Matthew 25:35–36). The economic blueprint in God's kingdom works against personal increase and selfish accumulation and works toward distribution out to the extremities. Perhaps that's why Jesus said that it was impossible to serve both God and money; people can't submit to the desire for personal accumulation *and* submit to the desire for God at the same time.[7]

Living productive kingdom lives requires that we change our habits and lifestyles. Junk food and easy chairs don't produce world-class athletes. If we jump into the race and fail to reorient our lives in tune with missional disciplines and practices, we will most likely fall out of the race completely, thinking it is an impossible and miserable task. But by retraining our minds, attitudes, and hearts in combination with actions and disciplines that are otherly oriented, we will be able to shape our lives into good news wherever we are.

— IDEAS AND SUGGESTIONS FOR FORMING A MISSIONAL LIFESTYLE —

*Examine your heart—*

- Prayerfully ask the Lord to search your heart in light of materialistic and consumptive habits.
  - » Talk about these issues as a family and with your small group.
  - » Don't fall prey to guilt. The Lord doesn't bury us in guilt. He brings conviction to our hearts so that we recognize our sin in order to get free from it.
  - » Pray for the Lord to give you wisdom to get untangled from the grip of materialism.

*Experiment—*

- (For families and groups) Go on a shopping trip to a few secondhand-clothing stores. Afterward, meet for show-and-tell, sharing what you purchased, what you learned, and what attitudes and feelings were stirred up in yourself.

*Lighten up—*

- If you currently rent a storage unit, empty it out. Sell or give away the contents. This will enable you to bless others and save money from the rental.

- Are you driving the car you *need*? Does your family have more cars than necessary? By downgrading you may be able to save money on car payments as well as insurance premiums.

*Budget for mission—*

I recall Tony Campolo once telling the story of his family budget. Early in their marriage he and his wife made the decision to live on a conservative budget in order to bless others. They chose to drive used cars and live in a modest home. Over the years they adjusted their budget according to the national cost of living, but in spite of Tony's fame and increased income, they continued to live modestly and give the overflow away. Today they live on about $50,000 per year and give the rest away. This would be a wonderful decision for young couples to adopt as they begin their lives together. It would also be a great decision for anyone to downsize toward.

>>> **6**

# OH RAAAAWWB!

## When Things Go Wrong in the Suburbs

It occurs to me that this is not a neighborhood; it is
only a collection of unconnected individuals.

Philip Langdon, *A Better Place to Live*

As suburban living surged in the late 1950s and early
1960s, the airwaves were filled with idyllic portrayals
of American families exercising their right to pursue
happiness. *The Adventures of Ozzie & Harriet, Father Knows
Best, The Donna Reed Show, Hazel, Leave It to Beaver* . . . it
was a full menu. Heck, even creepy ghoulish families such as
*The Munsters* and *The Addams Family* were represented as
well. Studios pumped out Rockwellesque images of the new
suburban lifestyle featuring television shows with squeaky-
clean kids and perfectly trimmed lawns. Housewives always
looked as though they had just returned from the beauty
parlor, kept a photo-ready house, had fresh cookies and milk
prepared for after-school snacks, and had dinner ready when

Dad came home from work. Commercial breaks featured the stars of the shows, still in character, plying the products that helped them live such a happy life.

Somewhere in our minds, though bedrooms were almost never shown, we had to figure that whatever did happen in there must be working pretty good too, because Dad always seemed happy. It was amazing how Mom put so much into her days, but still seemed to have plenty left for the evening. No pressure for the American housewife here, huh?

One of the most popular suburban-based television shows of all time was *The Dick Van Dyke Show*, featuring Mary Tyler Moore as Laura Petrie. Here was a "typical" housewife who just happened to look like Jackie Kennedy, dance like Ginger Rogers, sing like Judy Garland, and cook like Julia Childs. Who wouldn't want Laura Petrie as a wife? Though every crisis was sure to be solved in thirty minutes or less, they always began with Laura's signature vibrato cry, calling to her husband, "Oh Raaaaawwwb!" This meant something had gone terribly wrong.

Well, something *has* gone wrong in suburban life, and it's gone wrong for suburban Christianity as well.

## Welcome to the Burbs

I clearly remember the formative months of the church plant I led in the mid-1990s and pastored for the next ten years. Our planting team was moving from a small college town ninety miles west to the outskirts of St. Louis, Missouri. We were headed to the fastest-growing county in the state at the time, and the suburban landscape sprawled for miles and miles in cluster after cluster of subdivisions housing the 250,000 and growing residents. These new neighborhoods had names that made a person feel both safe and successful—Hunter's Glenn, Walnut Creek, The Vineyards, Spencer's Crossing, The Bluffs. This was the place where we would embark on our church-planting mission.

By this time my wife Sherri and I had three small children and we made the painful decision to sell our treasured 1966 Mustang coupe and buy . . . you guessed it . . . a minivan. For a thirty-year-old man, the phrase "Buy a *minivan*" is tantamount to "Eat your broccoli." Gag. This is the point in a man's life when everything changes. There's no looking back. He might as well begin to wear white button-down shirts, black horn-rimmed glasses, and get a pocket protector stamped "Vernie Keel Funeral Home." Welcome to the dweeb zone, buddy. All vestiges of youth are laid to rest when a guy capitulates and buys a minivan.

Our move was still a few weeks away, and I had not personally met a "specimen" of the typical person we were planting a church to reach. My first encounter came about as I replied to a newspaper ad for a minivan and drove east for two hours to check it out. It happened to be located in the heart of the area we were moving to. The directions given by the lady that placed the ad led me through a maze of concrete trails to a two-story colonial with sprinkler heads that recessed into the ground as I pulled up.

In the driveway sat a sparkling green Mercury minivan that was less than a year old. Just what we were looking for. Before I could even ring the doorbell, Ken and Barbie greeted me, although they used aliases. They were perfect. All that was missing was the pink Cadillac.

I was invited inside, offered a soda, and introduced to their two toddlers as Barbie shared her sadness about selling her beloved minivan. I told her I was even sadder for needing to buy it, and she tilted her head and looked at me like a confused poodle. Ken pitched me the keys and the two of us went out for a test drive. As we drove along, he shared with me the reason he and Barbie were selling the van. I asked him if he was tired of broccoli. He also looked at me like a confused poodle and told me they had recently sold their house, were moving to a larger home, and were anticipating some financial pressure. The increased house payment that came with the

## JUST SAYIN'...

Many—if not most—times when we purchase houses, cars (or a second car), clothing, and electronics, we are indulging in consumption of much more than basic needs. If we choose to be honest, the truth is, we are satisfying latent desires for status and identity. The pursuit of fulfillment and happiness through materialism is the driving reason behind most of our brand choices. This has much more to do with our buying decisions than the filling of basic needs.

—*Alan Hirsch*

larger home created the need to sell the van. They planned to buy something less expensive.

"Why are you buying a bigger house?" I asked. "More kids on the way?" I figured they probably were expecting their third child or at least were planning on having another one in the future. "No, that's been taken care of . . . snip, snip . . . you know," Ken winked and told me. "It's just that we've got a lot of stuff in storage, we're thinking about getting a boat . . . I don't know, we just need more space," he said.

I told him I figured it must be tough, having to leave friends from the neighborhood, but he said they had lived there for only about three years and really didn't know anybody anyway, so they didn't feel they were leaving much behind. Ken explained that they were moving into a new subdivision of executive homes in a gated community. The new house had 3500 square feet of living space and a three-car garage, while the present home had *only* 2600 square feet and a two-car garage.

The conversation eventually swung to my side as he asked what I did for a living. After I explained that no, a church planter is not a landscaper for churches, but that we were coming to the area to start a new church, Ken shook his head and raised his eyebrows, saying, "Good luck. You're gonna have a hell of a hard time around here because most people in this area are like me. They're overworked, in major debt, and don't have much time for church." I was pretty quiet for the remainder of the test drive.

Driving back home, the reality of this new mission field quieted my soul. "Geeze, this may be harder than I thought," I mumbled to myself. It was as if God was using Barbie and Ken as a wake-up call for me to know what I was facing. My vision was not to just grow a cool, large church (though I wanted a cool, large church). I wanted to reach people who were not fully engaged in following Jesus. I wanted to see them not only come to belief and trust in him as a savior, I wanted to help them become full-bore disciples, taking on the agenda of the reign of God—an otherly focused lifestyle.

It was at this point I began to realize that although the suburbs I saw with my eyes displayed example after example of perfectly manicured lawns, medians, and street corners, the spiritual fields were full of towering, choking weeds and thickets. Jesus' words exploded in my heart:

> The seed cast in the weeds represents the ones who hear the kingdom news but are overwhelmed with worries about all the things they have to do and all the things they want to get. The stress strangles what they heard, and nothing comes of it. (Mark 4:18–19 Message)

Looking back, I realize it should have been one of the top things I considered, but this was the first time I was confronted with the state of the church planting soil I would be working in. I was discovering that there is a lot of mixture in suburban culture that works against growing missional followers of Jesus, and the same principles that guide a knowledgeable gardener must be applied here as well—not the least of which is to know your soil. This is true for us all, as we develop our own walk with the Lord. Weeds, rocks, stumps, and thistles are all around our lives, trying to choke out the missional impulse.

## Planting on the Moon

When my wife and I started our first garden, we had a soil test conducted, and the fellow who reported the results said,

"You're trying to grow stuff on the moon." That's how bad it was. Our soil had a lot of clay and required us to till and mix in several additives. We made the necessary adjustments to the soil and ended up with a great garden. But the first vital step was for us to really understand the situation we were facing. It was not enough for us to simply plant seeds and hope for a harvest. Neither was it enough for us to have top-quality seeds or to faithfully water and nurture them.

In like manner, we needed a realistic understanding of the culture—the soil—we were working with. This is the situation facing suburban Christians and leaders today. Many aspects of the cultural soil in the suburbs are not conducive to generating a healthy harvest. We absolutely can develop missional lives in the suburbs, but we must begin by evaluating our "dirt."

Suburbs came about as cities mushroomed in growth, spreading to outlying areas away from the hearts of cities, and as cars became affordable for just about anyone. This led to designs that were not only car-friendly but also car-necessary. Today, if you want to live in or visit someone in the suburbs, you are better off getting there by car, motorcycle, bike, or helicopter. If you walk, it's going to be a long hike. Most suburban subdivisions have only one or two entries, as a series of cul-de-sacs are typically merged together to form most modern-day neighborhoods. "Older street networks such as grid plans, commonly used in development until the Second World War, have been dismissed by traffic engineers because their many intersections allow traffic of all kinds to flow on minor streets as well as major thoroughfares. The new street hierarchy—called a *sparse hierarchy* by some because it severely limits the number of through routes—promises more order and efficiency."[1]

The neighborhood I grew up in was based on one of the older grid systems for streets. This meant that a lot of pass-through traffic occurred. As a youngster in the 1970s, my friends and I had a lot of fun with the poor souls who drove through our neighborhood. More than once we pulled the old purse-on-a-string trick, where we would lay a woman's purse in the middle of the street at nighttime with nylon fishing line attached. (This prank is older than the whoopee cushion, but still funny.) As we hid in nearby bushes, a driver would stop and exit his car to check out the purse, and just as the guy was about to pick it up, we would yank on the line. This usually elicited a startled jump followed by a symphony of cursing as the guy with the *found-and-lost* fortune looked in vain to find who had just duped him. We would run and, laughing hysterically, fall into the tall grassy fields nearby.

The newer suburbs combine zoning ordinances with cul-de-sacs to minimize unnecessary traffic, making for quieter and safer living. Parents feel pretty secure in letting their children play in the cul-de-sac, as vehicular, drive-past traffic is minimal and most of the cars that do come through are carrying residents of that street. Drive through a neighborhood that you don't live in and there's a good chance you will interrupt a street hockey or football game. As you pass through, the kids will look at you like you're crazy—"What's wrong with that guy? Driving through here like that. It's like he thinks this a road or something."

In the modern suburb there is no neighborhood Starbucks or drugstore. Marketplace activity is funneled to shopping centers and malls. Grocery stores, banks, drugstores, coffee shops, pubs, and schools are located *outside* of the neighborhood. This means people don't drive *through* on their way to another place or cross through as a shortcut for other destinations. For the most part the people who drive there live there.

## Life in Silos

Prior to modern suburban design and zoning categories, living was done across a rather seamless landscape. People were significantly connected to others beyond their immediate family through a network of relationships that were formed as a natural by-product of daily living. There was consistent and genuine connection with others. People frequently interacted with one another as they walked to the neighborhood drugstore, pub, or corner market. As they were on their way, off-the-cuff conversations took place with neighbors sitting on their front porches having morning coffee or catching an afternoon breeze. This was just one of the ways people got to know one another. Over the years friendships developed and true community was nurtured and developed.

Sociologists have a term—*social capital*—that is a measure of the degree that people are connected in social networks, as well as the overall value of those relationships. Author David Halpern defines social capital:

> Most people are embedded in a series of different social networks and associations. We have friends. We go to work and mix with colleagues. We may belong to a union or professional association that keeps us in touch with similar professionals outside of our own work context. In our leisure time, we may play a sport with a particular group or club, and we may belong to other interest-based groups, whether this interest is knitting, model railways or astro-physics. We may also belong to a political party, or more frequently, to a pressure group working to save whales, the environment, or the right to carry weapons. And in our home life, we are part of a family, a neighborhood, and probably a religious or ethnic community too. These everyday networks, including many of the social customs and bonds that define them and keep them together, are what we mean when we talk about social capital.[2]

Social capital has waned over the years as relationships began to take on boundaries across the landscape of community cultures. Take the typical suburban neighborhood, for example. Neighborly relationships began to thin as central air-conditioning and television sets took their place in most homes. The front porch became obsolete as people left the porch swing for the recliner, developing "friendships" with the Bunkers, the Waltons, and the crew at Cheers. It wasn't long before zoning codes and cul-de-sacs made sidewalks obsolete and unnecessary for most suburban neighborhoods. They were no longer needed because there was no place to walk to anyway.

The term *single-family home* describes suburban housing pretty well. Each family has its own extremely private *silo* where family life is docked between activities in a variety of other *silos.* I use the term "extremely private" because this is the way most people in the Gen X and following generations look at their homes. This is especially true if they have lived most of their lives in modern suburban silos.

I have to admit this is the way I tend to view my own home. It's one of many issues on my "I need to change *this* about myself" list. My introvertish, more self-protective nature doesn't want or expect people to drop by unannounced. And years of living on cul-de-sacs have done little but feed my selfish side. But I've noticed that my parents and people from their generation usually give no thought when friends stop by without calling first. Many times I've witnessed my parents' friends drop in, unannounced, on a Saturday or Sunday afternoon and stay until late evening. In no time, my mother would have snacks and drinks out for everyone. One of the first questions she would ask is, "Can you stay for dinner?" Modern suburban life doesn't foster such a mindset of hospitality. Quite the opposite, it reinforces the desire for privacy.

A variety of silos serve as containers for commerce, employment, worship, exercise, education, and so forth. They are most

**JUST SAYIN'...**

When it comes to our houses, the mindset is that this is "our" space, and the people we choose to invite into this space are selected as to whether or not they will inconvenience us or pose a threat to our safety. Why? Because visitors stress us out. Strangers really stress us out. Though this is understandable from a cultural standpoint, the spiritual reality is that the family has effectively become an idol. This situation causes the effort required for missional hospitality to be viewed as a threat. Our cultural comfort once again trumps the kingdom—an idol is born.

—*Alan Hirsch*

always zoned out of the residential neighborhood. This results in a life that becomes *compartmentalized*. We live multiple *lives* (e.g., home life, work life, church life, exercise life) among different sets of people. So, the people we live near are usually not the same people with whom we work, shop, or worship. There is no genuine network of relationships, just *sets* of relationships. It all creates a mentality whereby our identities constantly shift and change in light of the moment or social setting.

Peter Block points to the findings of *Bowling Alone* author Robert Putnam and his research on social capital in Italian towns:

> His findings were startling, for he discovered that the one thing that distinguished the more successful from the less successful towns was the extent of social capital, or widespread relatedness that existed among its citizens. Success as a town was not dependent on the town's geography, history, economic base, cultural inheritance, or financial resources. Putnam shows how we have become increasingly disconnected from family, friends, neighbors, and our democratic structures—and how we may reconnect. He warns that our stock of social capital—the very fabric of our connections with each other—has plummeted, impoverishing our lives and communities. Geography, history, great leadership, fine programs, economic advantage, and any other factors that we traditionally use to explain success made a marginal difference in the health of a community. Community well-being simply had to do with the quality of the relationships, the cohesion that exists among its citizens. He calls this *social capital*.[3]

## Fragmented Lifestyles

For authentic community to marinate, we need a mix of people with various skills and interests coming together and rubbing off on one another. Silo living breeds social disintegration. It fosters a life that segregates our relationships with others and limits intermingling among the people in our differing silos.

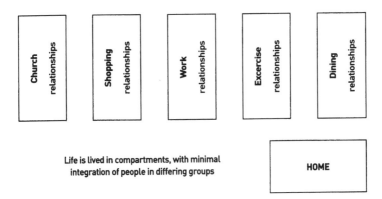

Life is lived in compartments, with minimal
integration of people in differing groups

Dis-integrated Life

Social disintegration dominates American culture and suburbs have aided in spawning it. This social pattern of *disintegration* fosters our lifestyle, which means that it is very difficult to bring the differing "parts" of our lives together. It's hard to integrate such a wide variety of relationships from so many differing compartments. Life becomes a churning machine, made up of many parts, rather than an organic and holistic body of life.

How does church fit into this? The people there are not the same people from the other compartments of our lives, so church leaders struggle to create a sense of community. There is very little, if any, social capital to begin with. In all the years I was on staff at churches and served as a pastor, one of the most common issues we struggled over had to do with getting our members to really connect with and know each other. We would host special events—guy's nights, gal's nights, single's nights, blue-eyed people nights, and people-with-tires-on their-cars nights—anything to get people rubbing shoulders with one another.

The most common community-building solution for many churches is a small group ministry. If it were not for the intentional and sacrificial efforts of church members who host and lead small groups, there would be virtually no semblance of community whatsoever in most midsize to larger American

> ## JUST SAYIN'...
>
> In an already overtly consumeristic culture, Western Christians tend to view the church as a place that exists to serve my spiritual needs. When viewed like this, it becomes just another silo. If one church (silo) doesn't fulfill my particular taste and perceived needs, then I will simply look until I find one that does. If this is true, then we can probably say that many Christians have now subconsciously determined that the "community exists for me," rather than the more missional "me for the community."
>
> —*Alan Hirsch*

churches. Still, very few small groups come anywhere close to developing genuine community. And almost every pastor or leader I have ever discussed the matter with agrees something is missing.

Most small group programs don't emerge from or foster natural relationships. The social "doing life together" glue is just not there. The frustrating thing is that many sincere efforts to create small group community come off as contrived and pretentious, often becoming just one more thing taxing our energy.

I believe the problems that come with disintegration feed a lot of the church shopping and church hopping that takes place. Most often the people at church are not the same people we are interacting with in our day-to-day lives. They are just the people with whom we are doing *church*. It's not as though our lives depend on one another (though they should). People tend to take the same mentality that the guy I bought the minivan from had toward moving from his neighborhood. Often people lose so little *relationally* when they move on, they can easily find another place to do church.

## My Little Town

Although I was raised in the suburbs of the Dallas/Forth Worth area, I spent a lot of time with my grandparents, about an hour's drive to the north, in a small one-horse town. The extreme opposite of the disintegrated life we experience today, theirs was a community with a rich mixture of integrated living. Era, Texas, was my favorite place in the world. To this very day if I'm drifting melancholy, I sometimes lie down, listening to Van Morrison or Paul McCartney, and daydream up a visit to 1972 at Grandma and Granddad's house.

Maybe you've had the experience of living in a small town or have visited a place where neighbors weren't afraid or embarrassed to borrow a cup of sugar, or on short notice to ask a neighbor to watch the kids for an hour. Era was that type of place. It was a town where everyone knew everyone's everything. But it was a good kind of knowing and neighbors not only were at the ready to share tools, kitchen goods, and a helping hand; they even (as late as the early 1980s) had a *party line* phone system. You had to be careful what you said on the phone because it was as good as tapped. Miss Elmira was a pro at listening in on other people's conversations without being detected.

Along with weeks at a time during the summer, I would also spend a couple of weekends per month at my grandparents' home. During these little visits, it was common to see my grandparents and their neighbors borrowing and sharing. In a typical week several friends would drop by, unannounced, to share a glass of iced tea or cup of coffee. Many times they would drop off vegetables or fruit, maybe a watermelon or a bag of peaches or pecans. During the holiday season, neighbors were constantly stopping by one another's houses to share baked goods. And great-uncles and aunts with crinkly faces like chicken-fried steak would supply my sister and me with those Life Saver candy books or coloring books and the fat crayons.

In a crisis people were *there* for one another. I was around one late-summer morning when the teenage girls from next door knocked frantically on my grandparents' front door. Their mother had been canning fruit and spilled a pot of boiling water across her chest, leaving severe burns. The family didn't have medical insurance and Grandma cared for her wounds and nursed her back to health over a period of several weeks.

167

The lone grocery store in town was owned and run by a kind snowy-topped man named Jack Alexander. Granddad plowed his cornfields in the summer and fall, and I still love the scent of butane because it reminds me of the smell that came from his John Deere tractor. Two or three times per week, Grandma or Granddad would walk "to town" and the half-mile trip always included at least three stops. First would be Alexander's Store to pick up various foodstuffs or household goods. Adjacent to the checkout counter was a small kitchen table around which a few old men in overalls usually gathered. Between chaws of tobacco, they would fret about the Texas heat, cuss Nixon, and eat MoonPies, washing them down with Dr Pepper with peanuts floating in the bottle.

Our next stop was the post office. I've seen toolsheds bigger than the little tan bricked structure that was run by the widow Ruby Hudspeth. But I loved to go inside and look at the bad guys posted on the wall and I always got to open the little brass door—Box 61—that was my grandparents' mail slot. Ruby was my grandparents' next-door neighbor to the west and she always kept a bowl of Tootsie Rolls and candy corn on the counter for the kids. There was no need for Twitter in those days, because Ruby always shared the latest and best details on the happenings in Era.

Across the lot from the post office was the last stop on the way back home. George's Garage had a single gas pump, a holdover from the fifties that still had the *Ethyl* sign on top. Outside, next to the door to the station, there was always a card table with a group of old-timers entrenched in a domino game, and George would look out from under the hood of a car and tell you if the fish were biting and what the weather was going to do the next day.

The round-trip would take about an hour and a half—ten minutes of walking, ten minutes of shopping, and an hour or so of conversations. This was just a way of life, and although my grandparents had very little in material possessions, they were rich in community and had very little stress.

Life is lived across a network
of people and relationships

Integrated Life

## Self-Reliance and the Nuclear Family

It wasn't until the mid-twentieth century that people began to transfer from one single-family home to another with the frequency we see nowadays. This phenomenon severed links to networks in neighborhoods, and families actually began losing stability along the way. Prior to this, the neighborhood and surrounding community network was considered to be a critical cog in the support structure for families. Families viewed themselves as integrated within the community as a whole. But unbridled individualism and consumption changed this notion.

Convenience stores and twenty-four-hour shops of many types began to sprinkle the suburban landscape and mindsets changed. Why bother my neighbor for a cup of sugar when I can be back from the 7-Eleven in less time? I would probably be drawn into a conversation with her, and who has time for mindless chitchat? I've got Facebooking to get to after I'm done with these cookies. And why would the neighbor across the street borrow *my* chain saw? He can get one of his own with no payments and no interest for the next eighteen months at the Home Depot.

Though many people long for Mayberry, the notion that my community relies on me and I rely on my community is nostalgia, no more practical than those Pottery Barn rotary phones. In reality, for most people, it is not a realistic consideration or pursuit. Interdependence sounds good in speeches and sermons, but the common reality in North America is that it's every man, woman, and child for themselves. It wasn't always this way. In fact, it hasn't been this way for long. Historian Stephanie Coontz writes:

> The expectation that the family should be the main source of personal fulfillment . . . was not traditional in the eighteenth and nineteenth centuries. Prior to the 1900s, the family festivities that now fill us with such nostalgia for "the good old days" (and cause such heartbreak when they go poorly) were relatively underdeveloped. Civic festivals and Fourth of July parades were more important occasions for celebration and strong emotion than family holidays, such as Thanksgiving. Christmas seems to have been more a time for attending parties and dances than for celebrating family solidarity. Only in the twentieth century did the family come to be the center of festive attention and emotional intensity.[4]

It may be surprising to know the nostalgic images we hold of 1950s families were actually new phenomena at the time. We think of them as the end of an era—the *good old days.* Truth is, they were the *beginning* of an era. The lifestyle of television families such as Ozzie and Harriet, the Cleavers, and the Andersons were a product of the postwar consumer boom. By the mid-1950s, about 60 percent of the American population was at a middle-class income level. Coontz points out, "The increase in single-family homeownership between 1946 and 1956 outstripped the increase during the entire preceding century and a half. By 1960, 62 percent of American families owned their own homes, in contrast to 43 percent in 1940. Eighty-five percent of the new homes were built in the suburbs, where the nuclear family found new possibilities for privacy and togetherness."[5]

Like a sideshow carnival barker, television and marketing voices promoted the idea of the single-family home and the nuclear family as the answer to everyone's dreams. It was a marriage made in heaven for advertisers, the textile industry, manufacturers of furniture and appliances, and the home-building industry.

Social workers endorsed nuclear family separateness and looked suspiciously on active extended-family networks. Popular commentators urged young families to adopt a "modern" stance and strike out on their own, and with the return of prosperity, most did. By the early 1950s, newlyweds not only were establishing single-family homes at an earlier age and a more rapid rate than ever before but also were increasingly moving to the suburbs, away from the close scrutiny of the elder generation. The values of 1950s families also were new. The emphasis on producing a whole world of satisfaction, amusement, and inventiveness within the nuclear family had no precedents. Historian Elain Tyler May comments, "The legendary family of the 1950s . . . was not, as common wisdom tells us, the last gasp of 'traditional' family life with deep roots in the past. Rather, it was the first wholehearted effort to create a home that would fulfill virtually all its members' personal needs through an energized and expressive personal life."[6]

Author Philip Langdon points to the influence of marketing and advertising industries as a strategic shaper of the American consumer: "Since mastering the basics of psychology in the 1920s, the marketing profession has spent several decades honing its ability to manipulate our apprehensions about our attractiveness, social status, and other attributes. The latent worries are stirred by seductive commercial messages whose underlying theme is: Buy or be incomplete."[7]

Today the nuclear family is king of priority hill in American culture. And American Christian culture follows lockstep, suffering the consequences. The very notion that Alan and I would call into question the family unit as deserving top billing will be viewed as suspicious by some and anathema by others. The accepted and engrained American ideal is that people can be healthy and whole by developing a single-family home, and *if* some degree of community building

**JUST SAYIN'. . .**

Dual-career spouses have become the norm in suburban America. Most couples work all day in pursuit of the cultural vision of the good life. The yield is an exhausted life lived in a houseful of appliances amidst alienated relationships. The enormity of cultural pressure and stress means that families have become highly protective. In *Untamed*, Deb and I point out that homes have become fortresses to keep the world at bay. Sociologist Christopher Lash calls it "our haven in a heartless world."

—*Alan Hirsch*

happens in the family's spare time (which they have none of) and with the spare dime (which they have none of), then that's just icing on the cake.

## Home Alone

The barriers we've mentioned so far are hindrances to relational connectedness and tend to subsidize and contribute to a lot of isolation. Couple all of this with the trend of frequent job changes, necessitating moves across towns or more often across states, and people are forced to start over in relationships of community. Stephanie Coontz observes, "People move from job to job, following a career path that shuffles them from one single-family home to another and does not link them to neighborly networks beyond the family."[8]

Most people would be hard pressed to provide the names and occupations of the neighbors living on either side of them and across the street from their house, much less other neighbors farther down the street in the neighborhood. Philip Langdon cites psychologist Philip G. Zimbardo, observing that "approximately 40 percent of the population consider themselves shy. If neighbors on the cul-de-sac do not want to become friendly with them or do not have time for socializing, the shy man or woman ends up more isolated than ever."[9]

It is no wonder that we have such a depressed and drugged society in the West. The US Centers for Disease Control reports that more than one in every twenty persons aged twelve or older currently suffers depression.[10] I'm no psychologist, but it is reasonable to surmise that the lack of genuine community and relationships beyond the single-family home are a contributing factor to the malaise of depression in our society. Other researchers have also determined that the pursuit of happiness is a race many Americans are losing and point to a lack of relational connection as part of the cause.

> Americans are less happy today than they were 30 years ago thanks to longer working hours and a deterioration in the quality of their relationships with friends and neighbors. And while the average American paycheck had risen over the past 30 years, its happiness-boosting benefits were more than offset by a drop in the quality of relationships over the period. "The main cause is a decline in the so-called social capital—increased loneliness, increased perception of others as untrustworthy and unfair," said Stefano Bartolini, one of the authors of the study. "Social contacts have worsened, people have less and less relationships among neighbors, relatives and friends."[11]

### Void of Social Dependence

Americans are noted worldwide for their fierce spirit of independence. This quality or character is both loved and loathed by Americans and non-Americans alike. It really is a double-edged sword. On one side, it is a source of innovation, perseverance, and pioneering. On the other side it boasts of pride, arrogance, and unbridled optimism that can lead to severe consequences. The degree of independence that is both accepted and expected in American culture cuts against the grain of the way most cultures exist. Stephanie Coontz highlights the malady of hyperindependence:

> The Anglo-American notion that dependence on others is immature, weak, shameful, or uniquely feminine is foreign to most cultures. In the worldview of these societies, independence is antisocial; expressing one's neediness, even codifying

it, is the route to social harmony and personal satisfaction for both men and women. The Japanese, for example, have a noun *amae*, which means reliance on the goodwill or indulgence of another, and a verb *amaru*, which means essentially to ask for such indulgence. Although increasingly there is a disapproving connotation attached to these words, it is not culturally stigmatized to emphasize one's dependence on others. Modern American parents teach their children that they can be anything they want to be; in ancient Greece, such overweening confidence in the individual's ability to shape his or her own fate was the sin of hubris, and it brought the protagonists of many Greek tragedies to bitter ends. In precapitalist societies, economic, social, and political interactions were not separable from personal relations. No individual operated independently of the kin group or the local community. Consequently, definitions of self were always contextual, because the self did not pick and choose relations with others; it emerged out of these relations and remained dependent on them. Independence was feared, not cherished.[12]

### Won't You Be My Neighbor?

Most American children of the 1970s through the 1990s started their day with the PBS television show *Mr. Rogers' Neighborhood*. The man with the toothy grin and the crummy sweater crooned the joys of his neighborhood and issued an invite to friendship, followed by a half hour of learning and visiting with different characters in his neighborhood. The same children who faithfully viewed Fred Rogers have discovered real neighborhoods to be much more difficult when it comes to developing relationships and daily interaction. Pastors, church planters, and small group leaders have also discovered how hard it is to develop community from a society that is not experienced in true community. We've just not been shaped for it.

If we are willing to take the risks that will push us into uncomfortable places of reaching out to strangers and neighbors we've not known closely, we can see great changes take place.

Dan Chiras and Dave Wann have researched and written for years about the joys and ways of sustainable living and development of better neighborhoods. Their encouragement is this,

> Where neighbors once lived in relative isolation, you can create security, friendships, interdependence, and meaningful social interaction. The cost of living will surely go down, over time, while the quality of your life and the lives of your loved ones soars.[13]

## IDEAS AND SUGGESTIONS FOR FORMING A MISSIONAL LIFESTYLE

*Practice integration—*

- Work on bringing cohesion into your life:
  - » Shop and eat at the same places. Purchase services such as car care, haircutting, and cleaning services from the same providers each time you need them. Call workers by their names and make sure they know your name.
  - » Start a game night, book club, or monthly recipe swap party and invite people from several spheres of your life to join.

*Organize sharing—*

- Create a neighborhood *Asset & Skills Inventory* for neighbors to post items and services they are willing to share:
  - » Construction and mechanic tools
  - » Gardening tools
  - » Vans or trucks—offer yourself and your vehicle once or twice a month for neighbors who do not own one but are in need of a truck or van to transport an item.

» Tutoring
» Tax preparation
» Minor handyman type of household fixes
» Office equipment such as fax machines or copiers
» Music lessons

*Foster neighborhood interdependence—*

• Start a neighborhood blog or Facebook page (easier option) where neighbors can list:
  » Job needs and opportunities
  » Babysitting needs and names of babysitters
  » Asset & skills inventory
  » DVD and book sharing
  » Book, movie, game groups
  » Neighborhood events
• Start a regular weekend bike ride among neighbors.
• Organize a summer "movies under the stars" series. All that is needed is a projector, lawn chairs, and refreshments.

# DOING SOMETHING ABOUT IT

*(MISSIONAL ACTION)*

## >>> 7

# BEYOND KUMBAYA

*House Churches and Small Groups*
*as Communities of Mission*

When the Holy Spirit transforms the life and practice
of Christian communities, they demonstrate that God's
promised future has been set in motion. The joy, freedom,
and wholeness of life within the reign of God can already
be tasted even if not yet fully consummated. While not
perfection, life within the Christian community reflects,
embodies, and witnesses to a "divine infection."

Darrell Guder, *Missional Church*

It was a crisp October evening and I was rounding third
base and heading for home. A close play at the plate was
coming, and as I got closer and closer I had to decide
when, and at what angle, to slide. The catcher outweighed
me by a good eighty pounds, so bowling him over à la Pete
Rose was not an option. Within just a few feet of the plate,

I could tell by the catcher's body language and eyes that I was going to beat the ball, so I decided against sliding. But he was still blocking the plate with his large frame. Running full speed, at the last moment I took a side step to the right and swung my left foot around him to touch the plate. Milliseconds later, my body would never be the same. My cleat skidded across the surface of home plate and dug into the dirt on the other side. I heard two loud "pops" and felt the most excruciating pain I had ever experienced in my life. It was as if a great white shark had latched onto my leg. A friendly but intense softball league game had become a nightmare.

As a young pastor with no health insurance, though the knee was swollen to the size of a cantaloupe, I tried to convince myself it was just a sprain. Sure, I was on crutches for the next week, but I was back to riding my bike twenty miles a day, and a week after that I even played a little touch football. "I'll be all right . . . I'm good," I kept assuring my wife. Three weeks after the play at the plate, and after half a dozen incidents where my knee suddenly buckled, dropping me to the floor, I was in the office of an orthopedic surgeon. After examining my knee, Dr. Yamamoto pointed to my leg and said, "I don't know how you're able to walk." With the last drops of machismo and optimism going down the drain, I asked, "I'm guessing that's not good news?" Shaking his head, he said, "You have a torn anterior cruciate ligament . . . [long pause] and a torn posterior cruciate ligament . . . [another long pause] and your cartilage is torn as well."

I thanked him and told him that I would have to postpone surgery, but my wife and I had wanted to know for sure what was wrong. Dr. Yamamoto shared that he was a Christian and knew that many pastors were on tight incomes. He insisted on performing the surgery for free. That was a *huge* blessing. Eight months of therapy later and, other than two long scars and a big bump on the side of my knee, I was close to normal. From that point onward I would never look at the following verse the same: "From him [Jesus] the whole body, joined and held together by every supporting ligament, grows and builds itself up in love, as each part does its work" (Eph. 4:16).

Though they are not seen on the surface, strong, healthy ligaments are a must. They hold bones in place and allow fluid movement. Without them, the body can't move properly. At best it just limps along. It can take a seat, but it can't participate in much of anything that requires *going*.

We have reason to be encouraged today; right across the spectrum of Christianity, there is an awakening to a mostly forgotten truth that Jesus came to assemble a body of people, full of his Spirit, that would move throughout every pocket of human culture, shining the light of his goodness and mercy. What we are witnessing is the manifestation of the verse above. The body of Christ, not just paid professional clergy, is standing up and *moving* with missional intention and having an effect. The ligaments are strengthening and the body is getting out of the chair (pew) and moving—a critical step for making right here, right now impact. While statistics show that fewer and fewer people are *going* to church, there is a transition happening where more and more of the church is going to the world, living out the good news of the gospel. In the West, we've just begun the turnaround.

**JUST SAYIN'...**

The "body of Christ" expression is much more than a memorable metaphor. We must bring all necessary parts of the body into the missional equation for the church to truly function as a body. To be a Christian is to be joined to Christ, and to be joined to Christ means to be joined to his church. This "body" can express itself in many ways and forms, but one thing is always necessary: it must be vitally connected to one another and to Jesus as the head to be the body of Christ.

—*Alan Hirsch*

## Body Building

In the early morning hours following surgery on my knee, I was awakened by a nurse who was bending my knee back and forth. Startled and in pain, I yelled, "What are you doing?" I was afraid she might be one of those middle of the night killer nurses and she was going to torture me before snuffing me out with a pillow. Without stopping, she grunted, "You need to start rehab." I declared, "No . . . I need morphine!" She went on to explain that the muscles in my knee would quickly atrophy and that I had to immediately begin stretching my leg to keep that from happening and to start the long road back of regaining the range of motion in the knee.

Look again at the verse above. Notice that the apostle says the body of Christ "builds itself up in love, as each part does its work." Love causes the body to grow in both strength and number. People outside of the body of Christ have the opportunity to see our love witness to the power of the gospel in two ways: how we love one another and how we love those who are not following Christ. They are both critical to missional faithfulness.

It might help to consider the following scenario: imagine if you were able to step out of your body for a period of time and observe your own faith community—say, your church, small group, or house church—from the eyes of a non-Christian. What might you see that would compel you to want to become part of it? Is there anything particularly unusual or remarkable that would cause you to say, "I've never seen people care for each other like that"? Scholar Norman Kraus speaks to the missional attractiveness of the faithful community of believers:

> In the New Testament, repentance means renouncing our old self-centered life and adopting the new lifestyle of agape (love) demonstrated by Jesus. This same community, which exists "by grace through faith," is also the community of witness. . . . It has the character of a movement always re-

maining in and for the world. Jesus described it as a "city set on a hill," whose light beckons and guides the weary, lost traveler to the security and camaraderie of a civilized society. In the city there was safety from the marauders who took advantage of the darkness to rob and kill. In a friendly city foreigners could find protection and hospitality. Thus Jesus used the city as a symbol of the saving community, whose light shines in the gathering darkness, inviting the traveler to find salvation.[1]

### Relearning *Koinonia*

People who were involved in the evangelical church in the 1970s or early 1980s will remember the word *koinonia*. It is a Greek word from which the English New Testament word for "fellowship" is translated. It was used a lot because, if for no other reason, it just sounds deep. See if you agree. If someone tells you, "We gathered in *koinonia*," doesn't that sound a lot more spiritual than if they say, "We got together for tacos"?

Even if you've never heard of *koinonia*, as a Christian no doubt you are familiar with *fellowship*. For the most part, fellowship has become little more than a label that Christians use when speaking about getting together. Just about any gathering becomes *fellowship* for us. If a group is planning to watch the Super Bowl together, the church bulletin will add the tagline, "fun, food, and *fellowship*." If a group of ladies are planning a baby shower, others are invited to "fellowship with us at Jenny's shower."

Fellowship is a good word. It's biblical and central to the lifeblood of the church. But it's a word we need to relearn, to redefine back to its original meaning. One of the most often quoted verses on fellowship is Acts 2:42, which says: "They were continually devoting themselves to the apostles' teaching and to fellowship, to the breaking of bread and to prayer" (NASB).

We can learn a lot about the biblical definition of fellowship by looking at the verses that follow Acts 2:42. It's not hard to see that the early Christians defined fellowship as something much deeper than getting together around a game table or having a Christmas party. "And all those who had believed were together and had all things in common; and they began selling their property and possessions and were sharing them with all, as anyone might have need" (vv. 44–45 NASB).

Two chapters later, in Acts 4, we see pretty much the same thing said again:

> And the congregation of those who believed were of one heart and soul; and not one of them claimed that anything belonging to him was his own, but all things were common property to them. And with great power the apostles were giving testimony to the resurrection of the Lord Jesus, and abundant grace was upon them all. For there was not a needy person among them, for all who were owners of land or houses would sell them and bring the proceeds of the sales and lay them at the apostles' feet, and they would be distributed to each as any had need. (vv. 32–35 NASB)

I've heard a lot of sermons based on Acts 2:42, but not many on verses 44–45 or Acts 4:32–35. What is it about these passages that draws such neglect? One reason could be that they seem to describe a commune of some sort. This is not the case at all. Both passages paint a picture of the selfless characteristic that marked the early faith community. The King James Version of Acts 2:45 says the believers "sold" their possessions. The English translation seems to indicate a *once and for all* action. But the Greek tense of the word effectively says, "They *continued* to sell their possessions." The message is that this community had a living ethos that caused them to respond to the needs of their members with every available means as the occasion arose.

Here we see the essence of genuine biblical fellowship. It is a deeply committed unity of comradeship. In fact, the word *koi-*

*nonia* is used in Luke 5:10 to describe the relationship between Peter, James, and John. The King James Version and most other modern translations as well say these three men were "partners" in the fishing business. The word used for "partners" is the Greek word *koinonia*, the same word for *fellowship*.

This sheds a lot of light on what the Bible is conveying by fellowship. We're talking about something way beyond warm fuzzies among a group of people who meet every week or so around Bible study and Chex Mix. Justo González points out the depth of biblical *koinonia* in the following word study:

## JUST SAYIN'...

We must recalibrate back to authentic *koinonia*. It is critical that we cease from our overly consumeristic propensity to pick and choose the Scriptures we enjoy and are comfortable with. Perhaps it is the ones we are most uncomfortable with that provide us a clue to the renewal of Christian community. True fellowship calls us to that kind of sacrificial sharing and a quality of our relationship that can truly be described by observers as loving community.

*—Alan Hirsch*

In Philippians 3:10, what the Revised Standard Version translates as "share his sufferings" actually says "know the *koinonia* of his sufferings." In 1 Corinthians 10:16, Paul says, "The cup of blessing which we bless, is it not a participation in the blood of Christ?" The term that the Revised Standard Version translates here as "participation," with a footnote explaining that it could also be translated as "communion," is *koinonia*. Paul's letter to the Philippians, which acknowledges receipt of a gift, begins with words in which Paul is thanking the Philippians for their partnership and sharing with him. In 1:5, he says that he is thankful for the Philippians' *koinonia*, and two verses later he declares that they are "joint *koinonoi*" of grace with him, that is, common owners or sharers. At the end of the epistle, he says that they have shared in his trouble (4:14), and the term he uses could be translated as "cokoinonized." All of this leads to the unique partnership "in giving and receiving" that he has enjoyed with the church of the Philippians (4:15), and once again the word he uses literally means "koinonized." In short, *koinonia* is much more than a feeling of fellowship; it involves sharing goods as well as feelings.[2]

True fellowship largely eludes most Christians. This has caused the church to lose something of its very essence, flavor, and power to transform and deliver the good news of the gospel. It's like a hollow chocolate bunny, promising more than it delivers. If we were honest, we would admit that, to an unnerving degree, we are not really much different from the bingo club down the road.

I once heard of a football coach whose team was a huge underdog in a big game. His last words to his team before they ran onto the field were, "When you fight an 800-pound gorilla, the way to do it is to walk straight up to him and hit him right in the mouth." We've talked about one of the huge gorillas we Americans are going up against—the consumeristic spirit of "me first, mine first." Living in genuine fellowship, real *koinonia*, is a step toward hitting this beast square in the teeth.

### Unfeigned Love

The early Christian communities understood that the new birth meant they were not born as orphans. They were part of a new family. Jesus said as much on one occasion when things were getting a bit dicey for him. His mother and brothers came to take him home, and someone told him they were standing outside, waiting for him. Jesus asked, "Who is my mother and my brothers?" He then pointed to his disciples and said, "Behold my mother and brothers" (see Matt. 12:47–49).

The early Christians understood they had passed from death to life, from the kingdom of darkness to the kingdom of God's dear Son, and they were not bringing their old life into his. That life was dead. They were not bringing their old sense of cultural "entitlement" into this new life. Those rights had passed away. This was a new society, a new culture, and a new community. To be in this new family meant you were no longer an *individual* but a *member*. Not a club member, but a body part, a part of the *body* of Christ. And if another body part felt pain, you felt pain as well, and you could no more ignore another member in trouble than your eyes could ignore . . . say, a torn up knee. The second I blew my knee out, my other body parts rushed to that member. Both hands clutched my leg and every nerve seemed to be screaming "Help!" for the injured member of the body.

Love is such an easy word to toss around. So easy, in fact, that we have cheapened it. I once saw two bumper stickers on a truck. The one on the left said, "I love Cindy." The sticker on the right said, "I love my truck."

**JUST SAYIN'...**

Genuine biblical faith in God takes us to a place that is beyond intellectual ascent and a mere collation of correct ideas about God. It transforms us into carriers and transmitters of the very love that rescued us in the first place. There is a clear and distinct connection between God and the lifestyles that should be produced from a living encounter with God. Middle-class culture is all too often contrary to the values of the gospel: the gospel brand of love directly challenges our consumeristic obsession with comfort and convenience and our middle-class preoccupation with safety and security.

—*Alan Hirsch*

I thought, "Wow. I bet Cindy is really touched by the fact that her cowboy ranks her right up there with his truck."

The precise phrase "Love one another" is used a dozen times and its essence is conveyed in numerous other ways throughout the New Testament. On two occasions the apostles Paul and Peter spoke of love that is *unfeigned*.[3] This is an old word that means *sincere*, or not faked. Love is a word that demands sincerity, or the opposite of hypocrisy. It means the real deal. Peter says we are to be "obeying the truth through the Spirit unto unfeigned love of the brethren."[4] A tangible love for the members of our Jesus-family is the only proper response to the truth of Jesus and the gospel of the kingdom of God. Eugene Peterson underscores this essence in his translation of James 2:14–17:

> Dear friends, do you think you'll get anywhere in this if you learn all the right words but never do anything? Does merely talking about faith indicate that a person really has it? For instance, you come upon an old friend dressed in rags and half-starved and say, "Good morning, friend! Be clothed in Christ! Be filled with the Holy Spirit!" and walk off without providing so much as a coat or a cup of soup—where does that get you? Isn't it obvious that God-talk without God-acts is outrageous nonsense? (Message)

## Who Is "Whoever"?

Anyone who has lived in the United States for long has seen "John 3:16" on a billboard, spray painted on an overpass, or on a poster board at a ball game: "For God so loved the world that He gave His only begotten Son, that **whoever** believes in Him should not perish but have eternal life" (NKJV). It's a verse we are very familiar with, to say the least. Let's look at another verse—written by the same guy—that most Christians would just as soon forget:

> But whoever has the world's goods, and sees his brother in need and closes his heart against him, how does the love of God abide in him? (1 John 3:17 NASB)

So, who is this *whoever* person? The "whoever" in this verse is the same "whoever" that is in John 3:16. And John (the apostle who penned both verses) says the same love that was believed on by "whoever" in John 3:16 must also be passed on by "whoever" to the other "whoevers." Otherwise, John asks, "How can the love of God even be in *whoever* in the first place?" He is saying that the same blood that gave us a new heart should be flowing through our hearts toward others.

Is this a penetrating verse or what? It delivers a clear message, bringing that "Who is my family?" thing back up. It reorients us to the truth that we are members of a new family, and we should have the same natural inclinations toward helping our *spiritual* family members that we have to our *natural* family members. A missional community does more than pray and study the Bible. It takes its cues from the Bible and incarnates the Word of God in the lives of its members.

Just imagine what could happen in your own church or small group if this understanding of spiritual family were adopted. Even further, imagine all across the United States, during the recent recession and housing crisis, if the church of Jesus Christ would have, en masse, lived out the pattern of community seen in the early church. For one thing, a lot of downsizing and ridding of consumeristic extras would have happened, not merely in the name of renunciation of materialism, but in favor of Christian community and for the glory of Jesus Christ.

Pointing to the following passage from Jesus' final prayer in the Garden of Gethsemane, Francis Schaeffer calls true Christian community the "final apologetic."

> Father, I pray that all of them will be one, just as you are in me and I am in you. I want them also to be in us. Then the world will believe that you have sent me. (John 17:21 NIrV)

Schaeffer says, "We cannot expect the world to believe that the Father sent the Son, that Jesus' claims are true, and that Christianity is true, unless the world sees some reality of the oneness of true Christians."[5]

## Missional Salsa

Missional communities are those that intentionally *practice* the faith. These groups agree on particular ways of engaging the world around them and how to "gospel" the community within which they live. But these are not linear steps. They are not hard-and-fast rules. These moves are more like a dance, a rhythm that provides a bit of order and direction for living, while allowing for improvisation. To make them into stringent rules would be to degenerate into dead religious rules of duty.

The most succesful missional communities are ones that commit to a set of missional habits. This is a way for each member to live out the apostolic commandment to "*provoke one another to love and good deeds*" (Heb. 10:24 NRSV). Michael Frost and his faith community have adopted five practices that form the acrostic, BELLS.[6] Let's look at them:

## Bless

They seek to to do three acts of blessing a day: one to a member of the Christian community, one to a non-Christian, and one spare. Blessings can range from a simple email of encouragement to a gift of some sort or whatever.

## Eat

They share at least three meals each week with others. Same deal as above: one with a member of the Christian community, one with a non-Christian, and one spare. The idea is that around the table, gospel things happen.

## Listen

They commit to at least one hour per week of listening to the promptings of the Holy Spirit. Some members have a prayer walk routine or a particular weekly time of solitude of listening to God.

## Learn

They commit to read from the Gospels each week in order to specifcally learn more about Jesus. The Gospels are always included in the weekly rhythm in order to constantly stay Jesus-centered. They also commit to read from other books of the Bible. Then they commit to read one other book, fiction or nonfiction. The only criteria is that it has to be good.

## Sent

They stay mindful of opportunities to engage in mission on their day-to-day journey. To do this they keep a daily journal of how they have worked with Jesus during the day, and how they have resisted Jesus during the day. This is a consistent reminder that they are God's *sent* people. They are a missional collective.

 **JUST SAYIN'...**

In *Untamed*, Debra and I issue a call for greater creativity on behalf of Christians. The Creator of the universe lives inside each and every one of us and is fully present in our communities. We should ooze with creative ideas for missional living as believers and the community of faith. One of the most powerful illustrations of poverty is seen in a person who doesn't have a dream, and therefore nothing to hope for—no creative impulses. We were made in the image of the Creator to be creative. Awaken the kingdom dream-capacities of the imagination. A sanctified imagination is a powerful missional tool.

— *Alan Hirsch*

Henri Nouwen said, "My whole life I have been complaining that my work was constantly interrupted, until I discovered that my interruptions were my work."[7] If we can just keep ourselves awake to the fact that we are God's good news people, life takes on renewed siginificance, every day. Much of what we call mundane and routine can spark to life if we will allow our imaginations to come alive in a missional orientation.

My own community developed an altered version of the BELLS practices. An element of our weekly gatherings includes going through the acrostic and sharing our experiences.

We usually do it around a common meal. It has become a highlight of our gatherings. Many times someone will share how something the Lord spoke to them during their *listening* time provided direction for blessing someone else. Often we've had members share that something they saw in the Gospels that week opened their eyes to a missional opportunity that sprang up.

## Missional Line Dance

Small groups and house churches have the opportunity to synergize their collective resources and energy into significant impact in their communities. Our groups should be dancing two styles of missional dance: the *salsa* speaks more to our individual missional rhythm; the *line dance* is about our efforts as a community working in concert. Missional communities prayerfully look for needs and opportunities to *be* the gospel in their towns and cities. This makes way for the preaching of the gospel.

The Renew Community, a church near Philadelphia, is actually a collection of smaller house churches. These decentralized Jesus communities participate in three rhythms each month—exploring, serving, and celebrating. Alan and I asked J. R. Briggs, the founder, to share about how his church dances together in mission:

> Our house churches explore the Scriptures together by looking at God's Story and how we fit into that Grand Story in order to join with his mission. They work to partner with an organization, school, or group to serve beyond themselves among those in need. And they celebrate together with parties, because Jesus said the kingdom of God is like a party. One house church partnered with a group home for those with mental disabilities. Last Christmas they threw a party for the residents and staff. A few women cooked a hearty dinner and one of our guys brought his guitar and sang

Christmas songs. Some of our folks spent time listening, encouraging, and praying with the worn-out and discouraged employees.

Everyone chipped in and bought the residents a Nintendo Wii game system, and some kids from the house church taught the residents how to play the games. A news reporter heard about the party and wanted to write a story on it. When asked what kind of church they were, they said, "We're a church that throws Christmas parties for those with mental disabilities, because it's what we think Jesus would be doing if he were here today."

Another house church studied Scripture to explore poverty and the role of the church. As they studied, they partnered with the soup kitchen/food pantry down the street. The director was invited one week to discuss the specific needs of those within the region and the practical ways the house church could help meet those needs. The following week, families with children in the house church helped put together food packets for the soup kitchen.

Still another house church has a regular attendee named Herb who has developmental disabilities. They provide rides for Herb when their house church meets and check in on him regularly. On a warm summer evening last year, they gathered friends in the park and threw Herb a thirty-ninth birthday party. Caring for Herb opened up opportunities for dialogue and helped us build trust with the county social service agency that provides Herb with help and guidance. This agency is now one of our church's official partnerships where we give of our time, energy, and finances regularly.

Mission is at the heart of the gospel, and being on mission together, especially as middle-class suburban dwellers, is another step toward keeping the consumeristic bent at bay. Shared adventures are like glue to relationships, and there really is adventure to be had, if we will open our eyes and ears to see the needs right under our noses.

My friend Tri Robinson tells the story of visiting with his father shortly after he returned from a fiftieth-year reunion

**JUST SAYIN'...**

There is a type of community that comes about when people share in a dangerous ordeal or a particularly demanding task. Certain sociologists have called this Communitas. It happens when people move away from their safe place to a place of risk together as comrades. Communities of the Spirit are trailblazers that take on risks for the sake of extending the kingdom of God. I like to say where the Spirit of the Lord is, there is adventure.

—*Alan Hirsch*

with his World War II bomber squadron. He told Tri that though it had been half a century since he had seen most of his crew, it was as if no time had passed at all, relationship wise. Tri's father said he and the guys were immediately laughing and swapping old stories about harrowing near misses with death as well as funny escapades. They also wept together as they remembered comrades who perished during some sorties.

Tri said he came away from this visit with his father amazed at the bond these men still shared. They had not entered the air corps in order to experience community, but community was what they experienced as a by-product. And after all those years in between seeing one another, they were tighter with each other than they were with just about anyone else.

## Living Stones

Welcome to the living Stone, the source of life. The workmen took one look and threw it out; God set it in the place of honor. Present yourselves as building stones for the construction of a sanctuary vibrant with life, in which you'll serve as holy priests offering Christ-approved lives up to God.

1 Peter 2:4–5 Message

The church is God's master plan. When we encounter it, we are coming across something uncommon. We are moving into spiritual territory. It is God taking residence in the midst of our very humanity. The Scripture above says that God himself takes our "common" lives, joins us together, and turns us into something he lives in.

A few years ago my wife and I built our own house. Usually when I tell someone that, they say, "You mean you were your own contractor, right?" The answer is, no, we built it ourselves. We hired out about 10 percent of the work and did the rest ourselves. The outside of the house included quite a bit of stonework. This was a tedious process of picking up individual stones, one by one, and trying to fit them together. Each stone was a different shape and size. I would pick up a rock, turn it this way and that, hold it up on the wall to see if it looked right, and then I either slapped mortar on its back and placed it on the house or tossed it aside.

At the end of the project, I was left with a pile of stones I had "rejected," as in the verse above. The apostle Peter says that Jesus was the rejected stone. God takes our lives, joins us around Jesus, and constructs a habitat for his own presence and glory. This verse wasn't written to individuals, it was written for the community of believers. We can't take this verse and give it a personal, privatized interpretation.

Peter is saying that God joins our lives together and we become a community of priests. And thank God, we don't have to wear those tight collars either. The Latin word for "priest" is *pontifex*. It means "bridge builder." A priest is someone who builds bridges for others to come to God. We are a community of bridge-building priests. Wow! Imagine that. Yes, imagine that!

>>> **8**

# Y'ALL COME BACK NOW, YA HEAR?

*Rediscovering the Joy of Hospitality*

Is there not a crisis of hospitality in our society? It is tragically evident in homelessness and widespread hostility to immigrants. But it affects almost everyone in less noticeable ways as well. A stranger smiles, and we cautiously turn away. In our retreat from hospitality, we find that even friends and relatives sit at our tables less often than they used to.

Dorothy Bass[1]

had never felt more vulnerable in my life. After two days of airports and 9,000 miles of flying, I departed a plane with three other Americans I barely knew. I had been to foreign countries before, but Kabul, Afghanistan, was the most "different" place I had ever been to in my life. The sights, sounds, and smells were all strange, but the most *different* thing about this place was the four of us. Eighteen months earlier coalition troops had entered the city, and I assumed we would see

**JUST SAYIN'...**

The Bible places enormous value on relationships, including ones outside of blood relations. The term *righteousness* is at core a relational one—it calls us to right relation with God, people, and creation. God calls us to a heightened sense of obligation and personal responsibility felt by people to both friends and strangers. Hospitality is a vital part of that—it is a righteous act. And it should be no surprise to us that the extension of the meaning of communion is directly related to the concept of gospel reconciliation. It is hard to maintain grudges against people when you sit down to eat and converse with them or have them stay in your home.

—*Alan Hirsch*

American military men all over the place. To my surprise I was wrong about that. Shortly after leaving the airport, we didn't see any Americans, or military personnel. After a somewhat brief, zigzagging, and bumpy ride, we were hastily rushed into a house in order to keep our presence in the neighborhood as undetected as possible. For the first time since deciding to make the trip, I began to question if the people back home were right. Was I crazy for doing this?

The hosts were not even home when we arrived, but our guide had a key to the place and we were shown to our quarters. The stark apartment building not only looked cold, it *was* cold. Just south of seeing-your-breath cold. Exhausted, I put on an extra pair of socks and laid down for a quick nap. About an hour later I awoke to the inviting smell of something cooking and went downstairs to join everyone else for dinner. I had been told that our hosts were Americans, but I knew nothing else about them. I brightened up when I detected a familiar Texas drawl, and they told me they were from Ft. Worth. Wow! The place immediately warmed up about fifteen degrees.

The meal was great and Bob and Jo Ann broke out a bottle of wine they said they had been saving for special visitors. With electricity available only a few hours per day, the rest of the evening was spent in a candlelit living room with singing, prayer, and sharing stories about our lives and what the heck we were all doing in this place. After I crawled into bed, I wrote in my journal that I felt so much better than I did a few hours earlier. My journey had just begun and the next couple of weeks would include trips deep into Taliban-infested territory, but a feeling of safety and calm took over my earlier uneasiness. There was something about my hosts that had brought peace and a new energy to my faith. Without mentioning it, they identified with what I was going through and did everything they could to not only make me feel at home but bring the presence of Jesus to bear upon my situation.

## Always a Stranger

> Therefore love the stranger, for you were strangers in the land of Egypt.
>
> Deuteronomy 10:19 NKJV

It is one thing to be a stranger in a place you are *vaguely* familiar with. Say, like someone from Southern California traveling through the Deep South. Sure, the Californian will need to get used to ordering iced tea by specifying "unsweetened" or "sweetened," and he will have to get used to hearing "Sweet Home Alabama" on every radio station at least once every thirty minutes. But at least he can speak the language, understand the laws, and be secure in knowing he is a citizen, at home in the United States. That can be tough enough. But it is altogether different, much harder, to be a stranger in a *strange* land. It is this idea that lies at the heart of the call for all Christians to live a lifestyle of biblical hospitality.

The roots of the church reach back to God's dealings with Abraham's descendants. Years of living as refugees in exile and slavery meant the Jewish people had often found themselves as aliens in unfamiliar territories: "The stranger who resides with you shall be to you as the native among you, and you shall love him as yourself, for you were aliens in the land of Egypt; I am the LORD your God" (Lev. 19:34 NASB). We need a renewed mindset that we are aliens in this world and citizens of heaven. When this begins to slip, we also begin to lose a kingdom perspective and attitude.

> But our **citizenship** is in heaven. And we eagerly await a Savior from there, the Lord Jesus Christ. (Phil. 3:20)

> Since you call on a Father who judges each man's work impartially, live your lives as **strangers** here in reverent fear. (1 Peter 1:17)

Because of God's grace in our lives, as refugees on this earth he expects our gratitude to produce hospitality toward other aliens as well. To lose a perspective of ourselves as aliens and strangers is to lose the kingdom paradigm that keeps us sharp missionally.

Time and time again I have witnessed that poor people are usually the most generous among us. I have delivered meals to needy families, and before I was out the door, they were calling neighbors over to share the groceries with them. Talk to workers at homeless shelters and soup kitchens and you will discover many of them were homeless at one time themselves. Their thankfulness and identification with the situation of others makes them want to serve.

Mike McIntyre is a journalist who traveled across America, with no money, relying on the kindness of strangers. He writes, "I walk on, wondering how it is that the people who have the least to give are often the ones who give the most." Quoting a woman who had very little herself but shared a bountiful meal with him, "She said, 'We don't have much, but we don't mind sharing what we have . . . I know what it's like to be hungry. There've been times when I've been down to my last ten cents, but people have always helped me.'"[2]

## More than Tea and Cookies

Words evolve over time, their meanings changing along the way, and *hospitality* is a word that has done so. It usually stirs ideas that fall short of the biblical meaning. Henri Nouwen suggests, "At first the word 'hospitality' might evoke the image of soft sweet kindness, tea parties, bland conversations and a general atmosphere of coziness."[3] I have to admit that although I've studied it quite a bit over the years and attempt to live a biblical version, when I hear the word "hospitality," I still wrestle with pictures of a Martha Stewart dinner party with fine china, mini-sandwiches, caviar, and crackers. Scenes such as this have their place within the concept of hospitality, but the biblical picture is far deeper and richer. As Nouwen says, "If there is any concept worth restoring to its original depth and evocative potential, it is the concept of hospitality. It is one of the richest biblical terms that can deepen and broaden our insight in our relationships to our fellow human beings."[4]

Almost every year our family hosts a Christmas party that everyone loves to attend because Sherri, my wife, is such a great hostess. She wants everything from the front porch to the back fence gate in perfect order. The buffet of snacks, drinks, and especially her famous eggnog is always both great tasting and presented as though they were staged for a magazine feature. Every candle must be lit and the background music has to be just right. I learned a long time ago to just shut up and do what she asks (tells) me to do as we prepare for the party. It took several years for me to understand that her determination for everything to be perfect at these parties was not because she was vain or felt the excellence or lack thereof reflected on her. No, her joy is in everyone having a great time and a wonderful experience. Sherri's delight is in bringing joy to our guests.

Biblical hospitality does carry with it the idea of being a host, but it is not limited to the "party host" concept. What we are serving is the good news of the kingdom of God. Everyone is traveling through a spiritually broken world. It is a hostile environment. The event we are hosting is life, everyday-doing-what-you-do life. Grasping a biblical understanding of hospitality starts with viewing ourselves as having a God-given responsibility for hosting life, right here and right now. It is especially tied to love for strangers. In fact, the word used in the New Testament for "hospitality" is the Greek word *philoxenia*, which is a combination of the words for "love" (*phileo*) and "stranger" (*xenos*). In line with the proposition that we have lost the meaning of biblical hospitality, Christine Pohl says:

> Today when we think of hospitality, we don't think first of welcoming strangers. We picture having family and friends over for a pleasant meal. Or we think of the "hospitality industry," of hotels and restaurants which are open to strangers as long as they have money or credit cards. Perhaps large churches come to mind, with their "hospitality committees" that coordinate the coffee hour, greet visitors, or help with the parking. In any case, today most understandings of hospitality have a minimal moral component—hospitality is a nice extra if we have the time or the resources, but we rarely view it as a spiritual obligation or as a dynamic expression of vibrant Christianity.[5]

## The Thing about Strangers

We have become good at taking a lot of Jesus' calls to sacrifice and risk and dismissing them under the guise of "being good stewards" or making statements such as, "It would be *unwise* for me to bring a perfect stranger into my home. He could harm my family or rob us." But Jesus said genuine disciples are to pick up the *cross* every day. The thing about crosses is that they are not comfortable. They are risky, heavy, and humiliating. The only way to get around this is to bypass picking up the cross.

The worst thing about strangers is that they are . . . well, *strange*. You don't know who they are, where they came from, their background, or their motives. For all you know that little old lady in Wal-Mart may be a real-life *black widow*. That bag of rosebush food she's buying may just be heading for the garden where she buries her dead husbands. The guy with the "will work for food" sign may be a professional panhandler with a late-model SUV parked around the corner. And that family a few doors down from our house? The husband seems a lot like the Randy Quaid character from *Christmas Vacation*. I wouldn't want to get too friendly with that guy.

Welcoming strangers into our lives and homes requires a lot of vulnerability. It pushes hard against our desire for privacy and safety, much less the inconvenience that comes along with opening our lives up to strangers.

**JUST SAYIN'...**

We should ask if our lack of hospitality is pointing to something deficient not only in our culture but also in our sense of missional obligation and therefore our discipleship. People should be able to experience a foretaste of heaven from our families and our homes. This is where the church can rightly be viewed as a community of the redeemed, from all walks of life. We must let go of the fears that restrict us. Visitors, especially strange ones, stress us out. This is culturally understandable, but we can't let culture trump our missional call. Missional hospitality is a tremendous opportunity to extend the kingdom of God. We can literally eat our way into the kingdom of God.

—*Alan Hirsch*

But here's the deal—our Christianity is not complete apart from obedience in regard to welcoming the stranger into our lives and homes. In fact, part of the litmus test for qualifying widows to receive the care of the church community was whether or not the widow had been prone to lodging strangers (1 Tim. 5:10). The same was true regarding who could be considered qualified as an elder in a congregation (1 Tim. 3:2;

## JUST SAYIN'...

I clearly remember when Nick Wight, friend and church planter, suggested that if every Christian household regularly invited a stranger, or a poor person, or a work colleague into their home for a meal with the family once a week, we would literally change the world by eating! At first I thought that this was an overstatement, but upon reflection we actually believe it is true. There are at least five million Christian households in America. What if each of these adopted the missional practice of regular hospitality? What do you think would happen?

—*Alan Hirsch*

Titus 1:8). Elders were expected to practice the act of hospitality—a love for strangers.

The great equalizer about strangers is that they always come in pairs, at the very least. One person cannot be a stranger. It takes at minimum two strangers to create the *stranger* phenomena. For every person I view as a stranger sees me as a stranger as well. So we are just as *strange* in the eyes of those we see as strange, as they are in our eyes. We usually fail to realize this.

When we welcome strangers into our lives, we are celebrating them as those made in the image of God and we are receiving Jesus himself: "For I was hungry, and you gave Me something to eat; I was thirsty, and you gave Me something to drink; I was a stranger, and you invited Me in" (Matt. 25:35 NASB).

### Hospitality and the Household of Faith

Regarding the lack of hospitality, even among Christians, Dorothy Bass writes:

Ironically, it is not just hospitality to the "stranger" that is in peril in our society. We are short not only of tables that welcome strangers but even of tables that welcome friends. In a society that prizes youthfulness, the elderly are often isolated from the affection and care of their own families. In many busy families, children find no after-school welcome home, and spouses find little time to host one another over supper. And when we become estranged—separated by grievances large or small, or simply crowded out of one another's lives—we all too often become "strangers" even to those we once loved. Can we move beyond strangeness and estrangement to learn the skills of welcoming one another and to claim the joy of homecoming?[6]

Hospitality was an extremely serious issue for the apostles. It was as vital to church life for the early church as, say, tithing or attending church services is to today's church. In fact, tithing is never explicitly commanded in any of the Epistles, but hospitality is, several times. Here are a few verses:

> Be devoted to one another in brotherly love; give preference to one another in honor . . . contributing to the needs of the saints, practicing hospitality. (Rom. 12:10, 13 NASB)

> Do not neglect to show hospitality to strangers, for by this some have entertained angels without knowing it. (Heb. 13:2 NASB)

> Be hospitable to one another without complaint. (1 Peter 4:9 NASB)

I know a professor at a major seminary, a world-famous author of over a dozen books, who had been in England for over twenty years and had never been invited once to any of his colleagues' houses for a meal. He had meals at restaurants with them many times, but never experienced hospitality in a home of the people he worked with for over two decades!

But is it all that unusual after all? Take a moment and think about your relationships in your current church community. Ask yourself a couple of questions: How many other members' homes have I been in, and how many people in my church have been in my home? Ask a few other church members to answer the same questions. Forget about extensive churchwide surveys. Whether you are a staff member or church member, the answers to those two questions are all the empirical data you need to know regarding the practice of hospitality in your church community. The contemporary church as a whole has neglected biblical hospitality. There is no one person or group of people to blame. As evangelicals, we are all reading the same Bible and have neglected the same portions of Scripture. It's not important to critique it to death. We just need to reclaim the habit of biblical hospitality and start living it.

## Opportunities under Our Noses

Opportunities to welcome others and practice hospitality abound, if we will only dream a little. Let's look at a few:

### Adopt Some Students

Gary and Susan are an empty-nest couple who are dear friends of our family. For almost two decades now, we have watched them be "Mom and Pop away from Mom and Pop" for several young people from the local college. The students are welcomed into their home on a regular basis for meals and general fun times. Gary and Susan have turned their home into a home away from home for hundreds of young people over the years. Gary's quick and corny wit and Susan's great cooking have made their home a hot spot for college students. I recently looked at Susan's friends list on Facebook. It is full of young people and past students who are now parents themselves who continue to share their gratefulness for Gary and Susan's hospitality in a time in their lives when they were far from home.

### Adopt a Grandparent

The nature of our culture is one that has caused many families to become spread across states. For many elderly people this means their grown children live far from them. This situation cannot only feed loneliness but also leave the elderly in helpless situations at times. This situation hit home for me personally. My family and I live over 600 miles from my parents, and they began to decline in health a few years ago. They were still able to drive and cook for themselves, but some things were becoming very difficult for them to handle. Pete and Debra Yabarra have lived next door to them for almost twenty years. My mom and dad watched their kids grow up, and there were always a lot of lawn chair visits between them and Pete and Debra. As my folks' health began to take a slow decline, the Yabarra family began to naturally take up the slack. Their son, Rocky, mowed their lawn, refusing to be paid with anything but my mom's home-baked pies. Pete took care of all the leaky faucets and general household maintenance and even installed a gate in the backyard fence that separated their yards so that my folks could come over to their house and spend time with them around their pool. Debra kept a caring eye on them overall. With us living so far away, this was an enormous weight off my mind, knowing my folks had someone watching over them.

### Adopt a Single-Mom Family

I used to tell my congregation that single moms are the modern-day equivalent to the New Testament *widow*. The early church was obligated to care for widows because they faced so many difficulties in caring for themselves economically and practically. Most single moms juggle careers, children, and finances with little to no relief in sight. Many a single mom adds higher education to the mix as the only hope for a better future for her and her children. Staci is a single mom who lives a few houses down from Steve and Jessica Mather, a family who decided to open their lives and home to Staci and her kids. Staci is enrolled in night school for nursing,

## JUST SAYIN'...

One of the weirdest texts in the Bible is in Exodus 24:11, "They saw God, and they ate and drank." One would have thought that eating and drinking were hardly appropriate behaviors for people who had just "seen God" but there it is. Isn't it amazing that all the covenants in Scripture are sealed around meal tables? The New Covenant no less! There is something theologically significant in this. Over time, what was originally intended to be a meal, with real food and wine, became the more symbolically abstracted Mass or communion that we now celebrate. But perhaps we are missing something vital. Communion, like all the sacraments, ought to be a missional practice because it proclaims the Lord's atoning death and covenantal love, not just to Christians, but to nonbelievers as well. And as far as the Bible is concerned, you don't have to be ordained to do it. Just have a meal with disciples and friends, remember Jesus and what he has done, and love on each other. Communion belongs to the people of God . . . consider yourselves ordained!

—*Alan Hirsch*

and three afternoons a week Bret and Jill, her elementary-aged children, hop off the bus and go to the Mather home following school. They share dinner, Jessica helps them with their homework, and the kids join the family in whatever activities they have going for the evening. Steve and his son Nathan maintain Staci's lawn and keep the oil changed in her car. The Mathers have been doing this for almost two years, and Staci and her kids are considered a part of their family.

*Begin Hosting "Communion"*

I am a self-avowed Mac-snob. After owning Apple computers for about a dozen years, the church I worked at purchased me a laptop PC, and later our children ended up with PCs as well. About three years ago, I went back to a Mac and awhile later my wife ended up with one and then we bought another one for our office. My oldest daughter had grown frustrated with her laptop and desperately wanted a Mac. One day I noticed she had found an Apple sticker and placed it on her PC in the spot where the

Apple symbol is found on a Mac. Not surprisingly, it didn't change the performance of her computer.

The operating system trumped the label. This is very similar to what has happened to the Lord's Supper, or as many early Christians would have called it, the *common meal.* We have reduced the joy of a bountiful buffet to a solemn ceremony around a thumb-sized wafer and micro shot glass of grape juice. As my grandmother would have said, "That's not enough to feed a bird." The lack of substance betrays the label. This is no "supper." There is not even enough for hors d'oeuvres.

When Jesus gathered his disciples around the table for the Passover meal, it was a visible expression of what was about to become reality. For hundreds of years the Jewish people had observed a feast that recalled the passing of the death angel over the homes of the Israelites who had sacrificed and sprinkled the blood of a lamb upon their doorposts. Jesus was the true sacrificial lamb, and he took the bread and broke it, saying, "This is My body which is given for you; do this in remembrance of Me" (Luke 22:19 NKJV). He was speaking of his body given as sacrifice for our sins. The next verse says "after supper" Jesus took the cup and announced it was the new covenant in his blood. In the ceremonial version of the Lord's

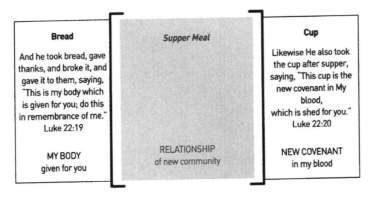

| Bread | Supper Meal | Cup |
|---|---|---|
| And he took bread, gave thanks, and broke it, and gave it to them, saying, "This is my body which is given for you; do this in remembrance of me." Luke 22:19 | | Likewise He also took the cup after supper, saying, "This cup is the new covenant in My blood, which is shed for you." Luke 22:20 |
| MY BODY given for you | RELATIONSHIP of new community | NEW COVENANT in my blood |

The Lord's Supper

Supper, we observe the breaking of bread and passing of the cup, but we ignore *supper*. In the biblical version, the "bread" and the "cup" bracket the meal (supper) of the new covenanted family of God. Our traditional version eliminates the center of the Lord's Supper and individualizes what is meant to be a communal celebration of sharing. We celebrate the bread and the cup, but we leave out the meal—the essential reminder of the new covenant community, the body of Christ.

In 1 Corinthians 11 the apostle Paul rebukes the believers because of their neglect and lack of caring for one another as it relates to the Lord's Supper, or common meal. He warns that they are eating the bread and drinking the cup in an "unworthy" manner and says they should examine themselves before partaking (vv. 27–28).

I have participated in hundreds of communion services over the years, and the majority of them are served with a warning for all who are about to partake to examine their lives and make sure their hearts are right and free from sin. This view of Paul's admonition is well and good, by all means. But by looking at the context of these verses, it is clear that Paul was also warning the believers to cease neglecting one another. Some people were eating before others arrived, some were getting drunk, and others were in conflict with one another. Paul was saying they were missing the point of the Lord's Supper. This was to be a meal of fellowship as the new community. The body and blood of the Lord had created an eternal covenant between himself and the family of believers. The apostle Paul points to Jesus' own words that the common meal is a visible expression of his death and newly established covenant between God and one another. Theologian Robert Banks says:

> Thus the meal that they shared together reminded the members of their relationship with Christ and one another and deepened those relationships in the same way that participation in an ordinary meal cements and symbolizes the bond

between a family or group. This explains why Paul does not direct his criticisms against the attitudes of people toward the elements of bread and wine or against the quality of their individual relationships to God but against their attitudes and behavior towards one another.[7]

Sharing meals together on a regular basis is one of the most sacred practices we can engage in as believers. Food is the product of our work, an extension of our very lives. Breaking bread around the table of fellowship is both a symbolic and practical witness of the unity of the body of Christ. By bringing the fruit of our labor to be shared with others, we are saying "my life for your life."

Hospitality is about making places in our lives for others. It is lived out on several levels and in many ways. It encompasses friends, family, strangers, and neighbors. It is a daily opportunity to practice selfless, missional living, allowing us space to show love and affirm the dignity of others, regardless of their cultural status. The only thing holding back hospitality is us opening our hearts, our arms, and our homes.

## >>> 9

# SALT BLOCKS AND SALT SHAKERS

### *The Power of Scattered Saints*

> The greatest need for our time is for the Church to be-
> come what it has seldom been: the body of Christ with
> its face to the world, loving others regardless of religion
> or culture, pouring itself out in a life of service, offering
> hope to a frightened world, and presenting itself as a
> real alternative to the existing arrangement.
>
> Brennan Manning, *The Signature of Jesus*

One morning I was heading off to my office and glanced across our yard, noticing our horses sniffing the salt block we set out for them. I don't know much about salt blocks, just that my wife said the horses needed one. She said they are used to supplement possible low sodium and chloride levels in a cow or horse diet. The idea is that the animal will have the natural instinct to know when it needs salt and will come to the block when the need kicks in. As I drove away, I thought to myself, "That's pretty much the way we do church." We tend to pack into church buildings (salt blocks) and say to the world around us, "Here we are, come and get it!"

Most of us are familiar with the idea that Jesus espoused in the *salt of the earth* metaphor. Salt has two primary uses: flavoring and preserving. It is the flavoring aspect that Jesus was highlighting. He was saying our very presence in the culture should cause the flavors of life to explode. Jesus was really saying, "Hey, disciples, you are to be the spice of life."

> Let me tell you why you are here. You're here to be salt-seasoning that brings out the God-flavors of this earth. If you lose your saltiness, how will people taste godliness? You've lost your usefulness and will end up in the garbage. (Matt. 5:13 Message)

The problem is that too often our saltiness gets isolated in churchy activity. It gets boxed up in the event or place we call church, and we have been conditioned to think that the main goal is to get nonchurchgoers to take a lick at our salt block.

This isn't to say we should not invite others to our Sunday morning gatherings. The issue is that Sunday morning success has become the *dominant* pursuit in the age of church-growth strategy. We have come to believe that the scorecard of success is based on how many people we can pack into the box on a given weekend. And we have believed that our primary duty as Christians is to make sure we are in that box on Sundays.

There was a time as a pastor that I would tell my congregation, "You catch 'em, and I'll clean 'em. Get your friends to church and I'll make sure they hear the gospel." It was as if we were working on making a sale, and the job of the church member was to secure the lead, then turn it over to the church staff and me to close the deal. I taught our members that all Christians had it in them to lead others to Christ, and in my head I believed that. But I must not have been so sure deep in my heart, because with our predominant emphasis on the weekend services, there was always an overtone that "full-time" pastors were the pros. We even made continual guarantees to our church members that we would not embarrass them if they would bring their friends to church.

This is the way it is in a lot of churches that operate primarily as salt blocks. Pastors and staff members knock themselves out, week to week, trying to offer the best experience possible for church members to get their non-Christian friends to attend. And I am confident that the overwhelming majority of these leaders have the right motives. We've all been trying to promote the gospel in the best ways we've known to do so. But I'm also reasonably confident this is not what Jesus had in mind when he talked about our saltiness.

Sherri, my wife, is fantastic in the kitchen and rarely does her cooking need anything but a knife and fork. But she always has a saltshaker set on the table just in case someone wants it. It's silly to think of her setting a salt block on the counter and telling the family, "If you need more salt, just go over there and take a lick." We don't go to the salt. We bring salt to the food. It is meant to be embedded in the meal.

## Think Outside the (Church) Box

Assembling together as the body of Christ is essential, beyond question. And when we do so, we should do it well. We should offer our best music, sermons, and welcoming atmosphere for guests and family. Many leaders Alan and I have worked with begin with a mindset that missional church means no church buildings. Some of them even demonize the use of and ownership of buildings and property. I certainly agree that a church building can be a heavy financial weight that can hamstring a church's mission. And in many cases our buildings have become comfort zones and safe houses from

**JUST SAYIN'...**

The prevailing approach to evangelism and Christian mission is for churches to develop programs, services, and events for the purpose of attracting unbelievers. There is nothing inherently wrong with wanting to be attractive, and we certainly wouldn't want our churches to be unattractive. The problem is that we rely on the gathered services to do the mission and evangelism—as well as the discipleship, education, and worship! To exacerbate the problem, outreach and "in-drag" has become the dominant approach to evangelizing our culture. The New Testament church was definitely attractive to its communities, but not from this perspective. Their attractiveness was in their living . . . in what we call "witness." The love and presence of Jesus flowed through them into the various societies and communities they lived in. The secret to their success as a transformational movement is that it wasn't a secret but a life evident to all (1 Peter 2:12; Col. 1:27).

—*Alan Hirsch*

the outside world. But there are ways that church buildings and properties can be used missionally if we will only think beyond ourselves.

The size or type of box is not the issue. I've seen plenty of house churches and self-titled *organic* churches that are inward focused and have no real missional ethos or impact whatsoever. Their members are not moving into the host culture, and they have just boxed themselves up in a smaller box and do church the same way, but now with poor sermons, bad three-chord choruses, and the kids shouting throughout the service. The issue is not about the church model or even the building but rather whether or not the life of Christ is getting out of the church box and into the culture.

Most Christians perceive the church service as "the main event" and thus the central locus for Christian life and activity. And they look to the pastor and staff members as being primarily responsible for organizing and conducting outreach and evangelism. As a result, the mission of the church is professionalized, and outsourced to the "clergy," thus leaving the majority of Christians out of the missional equation. This type of thinking causes the better part of mission to languish because it takes the majority of the players out of the game.

Too often, the largest portions of our time, resources, finances, and manpower go into one basket—weekend services. When churches focus the majority of time and resources in this way, we unwittingly quarantine the life flow of Jesus (the body of Christ), limiting our ability to reach the world around us. It becomes solely a "come to us" equation. In short, our actions say that what we do *inside* the building is more important than what we do outside the building. Author Jim Peterson comments on this:

> We recognize the importance of our gathering for teaching and worship, but congregating has the absolute priority as the predominant form in our churches. We are less clear that we are to live as a community in full view of and among unbelievers. If these were in balance today, the forms of our church would be different beyond recognition. It is just not a part of our tradition to plan for our being in the world with the same serious commitment, with the same disposition to invest people, time, and money, as it is for us to provide for our congregating.[1]

Peterson pinpoints the core issue. Jesus said, "Your treasure is the place where your heart is" (Matt. 6:21). You don't have to guess at what a person or group truly values. Simply observe the way they spend their time and money and you have the answer. I once read about an exchange between the legendary golfer Gary Player and the late Richard Nixon while they were playing a foursome. Following a perfect drive from the middle of the fairway, Player's ball landed precisely on the green, spun backward, and stopped three feet from the cup. Nixon said, "Boy, I wish I could hit like that." Player scowled and said, "No you don't. If you wanted to play like that, you would have spent the hours I have practicing. You would have hit balls until the blisters on your palms bled, and then you would have hit some more. You don't want to play like me. You should just be happy when you *happen* to hit a good shot." Player's point was that people pursue what they truly desire or value.

It is very much in the realm of possibility for our churches to start hitting better shots. Many already are. And Alan and I are cheering for more churches to assume the stance of a "going" church rather than just going *to* church. Jesus admonished us to go (Matt. 28:19). His model and instructions were never for us to primarily focus on getting people to *come* to church, the very thing that captivates the imagination of the body of Christ today. Again, please do not hear me as being down on "coming to the church." I am down on this as the dominant, almost exclusive, feature of church mission.

Being God's missional people means we put the wheels back on our Christianity. It means that our churches are known more for the presence of God in our people throughout the community than the coolness of our buildings, our billboards, or our polished Sunday morning services. This means that when people hear the name of our church, their initial thought is, "I'm so glad those people are in our community . . . we're way better off because of them." Our churches shouldn't be first thought of as, "Yes, that's the church at the corner of First and Main." Or "That's the church where so-and-so preaches."

A great example of a missional people from a large campus church is the Vineyard Christian Fellowship in Boise, Idaho. They have learned to utilize their twenty-two-acre property in several ways that have established them as a kingdom outpost in their community. Several initiatives of this fellowship reach deeply into the heart of Boise. The "Garden O' Feedin" is an organic garden, started and maintained by church members and community volunteers. This year's harvest produced over thirty-five tons of fresh, nutritious produce for needy people in the community. The GOF produces enough food to supplement the needs of the church's food pantry, which is housed in a large warehouse on the church property as well. The food pantry provides for hundreds of people each week and is an amazing ministry in its own right. It has an industrial-sized walk-in freezer and aisle after aisle of shelves stocked with food and household needs.

The Vineyard Medical Clinic provides short-term medical assistance for anyone without medical insurance. The doctor and nursing staff is made up of volunteer medical professionals and assistants from the church and community, including a translator for the Spanish-speaking community. A partnership has formed with Idaho State University that utilizes the clinic as a training ground for medical students.

A by-product of these ventures has been the development of relationships and partnerships with other organizations and with nonchurch members in the community that have volunteered to tend the garden, have worked in the food pantry or medical clinic, or have attended the junior master gardener classes offered by the church to the public. The Vineyard Boise is a salty church.

 **JUST SAYIN'...**

The prevailing concept of church, with its associated understanding of mission as something we do overseas, began in a period when the church had ceased to operate as a missionary movement. It had lost its true identity in the process. The age of Christendom has relied almost solely on evangelistic and attractional modes of engaging the lost. And it worked reasonably well in previous contexts because everyone was "within the cultural orbit" of the church—most identified themselves as culturally Christian. But that form of church is not up to the type of missionary challenge now presented to us by our surrounding context. Our present context demands more of a cross-cultural missionary methodology than the "outreach and in-drag" model. It's encouraging to see more and more churches that are coming to grips with this in America.

—*Alan Hirsch*

Many churches over the last few years have taken advantage of mass mailings, radio ads, and websites to make themselves known in their communities. There is nothing inherently wrong with these ways and means. Several wonderful stories come to my mind about people who ended up at the church I planted and subsequently came to faith in Jesus; and their journey began by hearing a radio ad, or they received a postcard invite through the mail. Many of these methods are well designed and very effective at reaching people who have Christian backgrounds or have reached a place of complete desperation. This may effectively appeal to 30 to 40 percent of the population *at best*. But what about the rest of the population? How do we reach people who are disinterested or completely turned off by the idea of church-as-we-know-it? This is why a missionary mentality should be the mindset of all Christians, everywhere.

## The Canary in the Coal Mine

In *The Forgotten Ways* Alan talked about our current condition in the West and how several recent studies and books point to a growing interest in spirituality. That is the good news. The not-so-good news is that these same reports indicate a waning interest in, and general feeling of alienation from, the church. Dan Kimball's *They Like Jesus but Not the Church* and Gabe Lyons and Dave Kinnaman's *unChristian* are recent books that speak to this spiritual climate. How we respond as the people of God should grab our attention. The most significant forms of church development over the past fifteen to twenty years have been based on what is commonly called the *contemporary church-growth model*. Alan comments on this:

> The more successful forms of this model tend to be large, highly professionalized, and overwhelmingly middle-class, and express themselves culturally using contemporary, "seeker-

friendly" language and middle-of-the-road music forms. They structure themselves around "family ministry" and therefore offer multigenerational services. Demographically speaking, they tend to cater largely to what might be called the "family-values segment"—good, solid, well-educated citizens who don't abuse their kids, who pay their taxes, and who live, largely, what can be called a suburban lifestyle.[2]

The type of church Alan describes here is somewhat effective at reaching non-Christians who fall within this demographic profile because there is a cultural fit and connection. These churches do not have to go into another culture or cross over significant barriers for the gospel to come across as meaningful. But what about people who *don't* fit this profile? By all accounts the church in America is in decline and Christianity has not bettered its reputation with non-Christians in spite of over forty years of finely honed church-growth theory and techniques. Our attempts at harvesting look something like this:

Population within middle-class cultural reach

Majority of evangelical churches designed to harvest here

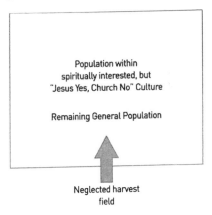

Population within spiritually interested, but "Jesus Yes, Church No" Culture

Remaining General Population

Neglected harvest field

Potential Harvest Fields

Churches that devote the majority of their resources and efforts to *church-growth* methods barely reach into the non-middle-class field. Like Nixon, every once in a while they hit a nice shot . . . mostly by accident.

### Shake It Up, Baby

Saltshakers have lots of looks and come in various sizes and shapes, but they are all based on a simple concept. They exist to scatter and spread seasoning over a broad surface. To be God's salty people, we don't have to abandon church, per se, but we must think beyond the boxes and blocks of our church events and buildings. Our imaginations have become captive to the *gathering* mode, to the detriment of God's missional purposes in and through our own lives. This is one case where it is good to be *scatterbrained*. As Christ followers we must never lose our habit of *coming* and gathering in fellowship (something the writer of Hebrews warns against—Heb. 10:25). I think it's safe to say we have that discipline down pretty well. But we must recover something that is sorely missing, a vision of *going* out in mission—of mission as *lifestyle*.

Recapturing the ethos and impulse of a missionary means we can't continue relying primarily on programs, events, and advertising to attract people to *come* to us. This is tied to what Alan calls *missional-incarnational*. It's about relating to people on their own turf without centralizing our expression as the people of God within the walls of a church building. Gregory Leffel, missiologist and cofounder of the missional community Communality, conveys the idea:

> It means, fundamentally, to be for others, to plunge into their passionate world—individually as mediators for the lost and collectively as a body locked in loving embrace with the world in order to save it. It means to identify with it, to be colored by its colors, to sense what it senses, to understand it from the inside in order to intervene in its thought-life and direct it to God. It means that the church must incarnate itself in the world, as Christ did in becoming one of us and offering his life to us as a servant.[3]

The root word for "mission" in Latin (*missio*) is the same root from which we get the word "missile." It is something that is *sent*. The heartbeat of the missional life is in its nature as one that is *sent* through incarnation. I love the way Eugene Peterson paraphrases it: "The Word became flesh and blood, and moved into the neighborhood" (John 1:14 Message).

This is the heart of what it means to be *missional-incarnational*. It is a "simple to understand but costly to follow" first step. God began initiating redemption first by becoming one of us. Jesus lived *among* us. He ate, drank, dressed, worked, sweat, took vacations . . . he did it all. He wove his own life into the fabric of the community and engaged its humanness at the most base levels. And he did it for thirty years before he ever even "went public" with his ministry. Imagine that. I know from experience with church planters across many denominational and organizational lines that most of them would be cut off from support and funding if they had not produced substantial "fruit" in thirty months, much less thirty years.

One of the things St. Louis, Missouri, is famous for is beer. Breweries, microbreweries, and pubs dot the urban and near-urban landscape. Awhile back, a group from Journey Church sought to reach out to folks who frequent such spots. They approached the owners of Schlafly Bottleworks, a local brewery and pub, and received permission to begin a forum called Theology At The Bottleworks. The monthly event hosts discussions on topics such as poverty, global warming, race relations . . . just about anything headlining today's culture concerns. Their mission is to open the eyes of people to see God at work in the culture and to develop relationships with non-Christians along the way. This ministry has been featured on many national media platforms and has received a lot of criticism from members of its own denomination. They have been vilified for not sharing the "gospel message" and have been heavily criticized for "having church where beer is served."

The critics of this mission have either forgotten or most probably have never learned that Jesus' ministry was em-

**JUST SAYIN'...**

It takes a genuine identification and authentic affinity with those we are hoping to reach when they are outside the faith. This is critical to acting incarnationally. It almost always should include moving geographically and initiating a real and abiding presence among the people group. By becoming one of us, God gave us the prototype for what human living and human community is to look like. By entering into the depths and reality of our world and our life, redemption entered into the heart of humanity. This was the way the Father sent Jesus and it is the way he sends us. This model neither needs to be nor can be improved upon. It simply needs to be acted upon.

—*Alan Hirsch*

bedded deeply among "bottle-works" type people. And he received criticism and eventually crucifixion for his trouble.

I have a Facebook "friend" who posts daily comments or links to news stories that are of an "*us* versus *them*" tone. His posts consistently rail against gay people, Democrats, and others who don't fit his notion of American evangelical "orthodoxy." He uses lots of phrases and labels such as "burn in hell," "uncircumcised Philistines," "lying Muslims," and "ignorant ungodly fools." This is grievous because it is an affront to the gospel message. I hate to admit it, but he reflects the mentality of a tremendous number of Christians. They view people who are of other faiths or are living nonbiblical lifestyles as enemies or filthy entities who are to be avoided and are fair game for derision or insult. These attitudes sully the name of Christ and patently deny his very character and message as "friend of the outcast and sinner." It's a sad reality that the fact that Jesus was labeled as a friend of sinners is lost on so many evangelicals. We should hope to be accused of the same thing.

Jesus wasn't just courteous to the ones whom the religious community despised the most; he was downright engaging and relational with them. To hang around with tax collectors and prostitutes was as bad as you could get in the eyes of the religious establishment. I don't think it's far-fetched to believe that if Jesus were walking our streets today, many Christians would call him a beer-drinking friend of homosexuals and gangbangers.

By telling us to "go into all the world," Jesus was placing the responsibility upon us, his disciples, to gain proximity to those who are not Christians. It is up to *us* to move toward them. Jesus didn't demand relationship on religious terms. His terms of relationship were the terms of the kingdom of God. And the constant in the kingdom is the pursuit of redemption and reconciliation for people and all of creation.

## A Scattered Mind

Contrary to what we might think, Jesus shows us that meeting *needs* is not the starting point for incarnational mission. John Hayes, who has spent over three decades serving and living among the poor in the most downtrodden neighborhoods in places such as Los Angeles, San Francisco, and London, says, "When missionaries start with the need, hoping they will one day get to know poor people personally, they are likely to be found 10 years later, still addressing the need."[4]

It is one thing to put on sanitary gloves and give handouts to those in need. It is altogether different to rub shoulders and live among them. One of the young missional leaders doing this very thing is Aaron Snow. In the last four years he has led the establishment of missional communities in Fort Worth and Las Vegas. Although he is only twenty-five years old, Aaron and his wife Morgan have recently moved to their third major city (Austin, Texas) where they are establishing another missional community. Read Aaron's own words on what they have learned about the importance of presence as it plays into incarnational mission:

> We began as a group of white, middle-class, suburban church kids that had been exploring what life as a follower of Christ

should look like. We started taking regular trips to the streets of Fort Worth and became students of those who had served there for many years, as well as the homeless individuals we sought to serve. It didn't take long to realize the abundance of tangible resources available to the homeless in that area. Churches and various non-profit and government organizations were doing a great job of meeting the basic needs of the people on the street. They did not need our Wendy's dollar menu burgers, or our hand-me-down fashion from the closet.

Not long after we began going into Fort Worth we met Michael Hatcher. He had been serving these people for years and began to mentor and teach us about working among the homeless. He and his family had moved into the neighborhood several years before and Michael was known on the streets as "The Rev." He walked the streets during the week ministering to these people and helped them get their ID's, jobs, and bus passes. But most importantly he gave them *himself* as a friend. We began to follow suit, learning to listen. Conversations led to prayer, topped with hugs, and a sense of comfort among the homeless; knowing they had made new friends. We came to understand that many of these people had not engaged in genuine conversation with non-homeless people in years.

We were seeing fruit from our labor but something was missing. While we had close relationships with our new friends on the street we could not truly relate to them. We began praying that God would provide a house for communal living among the poor. We were just 15 college-aged kids but we began to make quite the impact on East Lancaster. We had organized the annual "Art-n-the Park" celebration, birthed the "Unity in the Community Network" of organizations who served among the homeless in Ft. Worth, and had the attention of many in the city but we still felt we had so much to learn.

We found two duplexes on the same property. Two of the four units were for rent, and they were cheap. By this point our organization, *Intentional Gatherings*, had gained its non-profit status, and donations were coming in from people who believed in the vision of the "I.G. House." We moved two guys into one unit and four girls into the other. It was then that we truly began to learn the *in's and out's* of homelessness, and how to attack the problem at the root.

We were in a neighborhood about a mile from the "leper colony," which was full of the "working poor." (Those who are not-yet-homeless, but hanging on by a thread.) Our primary focus shifted from the already homeless to the almost homeless. The work among the already homeless continued and the relationships that had been made were fostered. The "I.G. House" crew grew close as they lived in tight-knit Gospel centered community, and sought to make a difference in the neighborhood in which they resided. As the crew grew they eventually took over three of the four units on the property. From weekend kickball tournaments to front porch after-school tutoring & Saturday morning breakfast in the yard our group of missionaries was serving Jesus in a way previously foreign to us all.[5]

## Sub-Missional

What if the Lord hasn't called you to live in a downtrodden urban area? What if you are called by God to live in the suburbs? God is the original missionary, and with half of all Americans living in the suburbs, you can be sure he has *sent* his people into the suburbs as salt and light. If you live in the suburbs, God didn't park you there to live the "American Dream." Rather, he *sent* you there to be a sign and foretaste of the kingdom of God. Many times mission remains on the shelf because of our perception that if we can't do something huge and spectacular, then our role is just to faithfully attend church, pay our tithes, and listen to Christian radio. Nothing could be further from the truth.

In the mid-90s our family moved into a suburban home in a subdivision that was about eight or nine years old. We were the proverbial new kids on the block, and not only were we hoping to develop friendships with our neighbors, we also

**JUST SAYIN'...**

The gospel and the conversion process always travels along relational lines and through the fabric of a culture. True Jesus movements always practice "planting the gospel" within a people and then allow the church to emerge from an authentic encounter with Jesus. In this way, the tribe or people group are changed by Jesus from the inside. Once the gospel is embedded, the church naturally emerges as disciples seek to gather in worshiping communities that are culturally consistent with who they are. This is incarnational mission and it really changes everyone on both sides of the equation—the sent one as well as the receiver.

—*Alan Hirsch*

wanted to be salt and light. I have had enough airplane conversations with strangers to know that, "Hi, my name is Lance, I'm a pastor," is not the way to get a relationship started with most people. I wasn't ashamed or planning to hide the fact that I was a pastor. But I hoped to get to know some guys in the neighborhood before I was typecast with all the assumptions that come when someone discovers you are an evangelical Christian . . . much less a pastor.

These were the days before just about everyone had a large-screen television, and I had one. We moved in a week before football season began, so I created some flyers and took them door-to-door. It was a brief introduction of our family and myself with an invitation for the man of the house to watch Monday Night Football at our house. The flyer said that I would provide snacks and for each guy to bring his own beverage of choice. I had never done anything like this before and had no clue as to what the results would be. It seemed a little weird, but I thought, "Just go for it!"

To my surprise a half dozen guys showed up. The next week they showed up again. Over that first season we became friends and continued our Monday night group over the next six years I lived in the neighborhood. Out of the six guys, one guy who had grown up in church but had not been back since he started college began to come to our church. Another one of the guys ended up coming to faith in Christ. I had shared the faith with Jeff on more than one occasion, but I wasn't the one to "lead" him to the Lord in the traditional sense, and Jeff and his family didn't start coming to my church. They joined a church they had been invited to by the friend who had prayed with him when he made a decision to give his life to the Lord.

Shortly after this decision, Jeff excitedly told me about his new life and shared with me that our family had spoken volumes to him by the way we lived. He brought up the time we had collected funds to repair the air-conditioning system of the single mom of four kids who lived on our street, the way our family helped his family out when his wife had a baby, and the fact that I had always treated him as a friend though he was far from Christ. He said this had impacted him greatly and sowed seeds and watered them prior to him deciding to follow Christ.

## Planting and Watering

In a scene from *Seinfeld*, George and his girlfriend are at the diner as he pays for a "Big Salad" to take to Elaine who is to meet them at Jerry's apartment. George's girlfriend happens to hand the salad to Elaine as they walk into the apartment and Elaine thanks her for it. George begins to seethe inside and eventually erupts in anger at his girlfriend for not giving him credit for buying the Big Salad.

This story reminds me of the way many of us have conceptualized what it means to deliver the gospel. The apostle Paul taught that the most important part of the harvest is not just the final step of plucking the ripened fruit . . . or delivering the Big Salad. Sometimes we plant the gospel seed and sometimes we water it. At other times we may be present at the moment someone says "I now believe in Jesus" for the first time. But it is all part of the process, and each role is every bit as important as the other.

For several years I have watched my friend Ken Smith express his life with the heart and mind of a missionary. He is not particularly articulate, sometimes dresses like Larry the Cable Guy, and you would never get him behind a pulpit. But it would be impossible for me to tell all the stories of the people whom Ken has impacted as he goes about his "normal" life. He runs a handyman service and once told me that his approach to each job is that he is there as a missionary, and if the repair job gets done, then that is just extra.

Ken has a habit of giving strangers rides when he sees a car broken down or someone walking along the highway. One day I asked him about this and if he was not a little afraid that he might be picking up Jason, or Freddy Krueger. He said, "I try to be careful and I won't pick someone up who is carrying an ax or a chain saw." Then he gave a more serious answer:

> I'm not the kind of guy who is going to teach a Bible study and I'm not what you would call an evangelist, although I have prayed with people to receive Christ. I'm more of a seed and water guy. I just try to think what I would want someone to do for me if I were in that situation. Just the other day I saw a young man walking in the direction of the local high school and I offered him a ride. On the way I asked him how he was doing and he said, "Okay . . . I guess." I asked him what he meant by that and he began to tell me about problems his parents were having and how things at home were not too good. When we pulled up to the school, I asked him if I could pray for him. He said, "Yeah, sure," and I prayed for him right there.

After learning about yet another person that Ken and his wife Candi had opened their home to, I asked Ken what thought process he and Candi have when considering opening their home up for others. Without hesitation he said, "Look, everything I have belongs to God. If I hear about someone who needs a place to stay and I have an extra bedroom, there's not much to pray about. I have a spare car that I have loaned out several times when someone needed one. I'm just responding to the grace God has poured out on my life. I'm not trying to earn my salvation. I'm just living it out."

# DEBRIEFING

## RIGHT NOW

# RECOVERING MISSIONAL MOXIE

## ALAN HIRSCH

That which you wish to change, you must first love.
Martin Luther King Jr.

I will build my church, and the gates of Hades will not
prevail against it
Jesus (Matt. 16:18)

B y now the reader will have gotten the impression that
my role is to be the missional conscience providing the
more theoretical framework for missional living right
here, right now. While it's true I am deliberately playing a
somewhat geeky role, and that I often sound somewhat theoretical, make no mistake, I really do believe that it is due to
our largely unreflective approaches to church, mission, and
evangelism that we have found ourselves beached on the shores
of the twenty-first century. These ideas need to be prayerfully
wrestled with, and integrated, if we are going to faithfully
negotiate the complexities of this century. The way we think of

ourselves and conceive our most basic purposes in this world make a massive difference in the way we behave. For good or for ill, *ideas have consequences*. I always remind myself of Einstein's famous dictum when he said that the problems of the world cannot be resolved by the same kind of thinking that created them in the first place. The truth is that we do need the wrestling and the reframing, and to do that we need to *think differently* about our tasks. For sure, we are going to have to repent of our ways—but that's a good thing.

I believe so deeply in the power of God's good news people that I have committed my life to somehow awakening this now sleeping giant. If we, the people of God, can "find ourselves" again, right here, right now, in *this* time and place, then the most profound of revolutions is on! And right now, we have a good chance of it, but for Western Christianity at least, it might well be our last chance to get it right—witness the now almost complete demise of *biblical* Christianity in Western Europe!

I will go further and say that the battle for the future of Christianity in the West will be worked out in America—and I say this as a non-American, an Aussie with South African roots and a deep Jewish heritage. If we fail *right here, right now*, in America, then I really fear the eventual passing of a vibrant biblical Christianity in Western contexts. And so, I have left kith and kin and come to America to help awaken the sleeping giant of God's people. I am, at core, an activist and not a theoretician! I am a stakeholder who has played all his cards on this time and this place, on the belief that it is a strategic time, a time when our choices are really going to matter.

To awaken the people of God to their dormant potentials, we have to shake off certain ways of imagining ourselves that hinder and therefore bind us from being the people we were designed to be. Truth is, we have all drunk so deeply from institutional wells of thinking about Christianity that it is hard to think of ourselves differently. We have, to co-opt Marx's words, taken a big dose of what he called "the opiate of the people"—*religion* (in the really bad sense of the word). Marx saw religion as the cultural force that kept people docile and submissive to the prevailing order of reality, and to be honest, in this at least, I think he was right. Use your imaginations here: morphine or heroin is an opiate (opium-based drug). Ever seen a person taking a hit of heroin? I have, and they effectively go into a deep, trancelike sleep. Religion does that to us . . . it dulls us and puts us to sleep. We become ineffective.

The good news is that the Way of Jesus was never the way of "religion." In fact, Jesus reserves his harshest possible condemnations for the very "religious" people of his day and condemned religion for what it does to people—just read Matthew 23 for a taster. Far from being a toxic hit of heroin, Jesus was a sobering splash of bracing, icy water! He awoke people to God, kingdom, their own potentials, and he started a movement that swept out from backwater Judea to utterly transform the world of its day. Everyone who was touched and transformed by Jesus was able to, in turn, participate in the transformation of others around about them. The Jesus movement that emerged from the dusty boondocks of the Roman Empire has swelled through history to transform billions of lives, and it still does, as millions are added every year.

*This* is the power of people movement, and *this* is the church that Jesus designed to change the world—a thoroughgoing people movement that had little of what we normally conceive of as what constitutes a "church"—buildings, clergy, bookstores, seeker-sensitive services, priest-run liturgies, complex theological formulas, or whatever. In fact, this very question provided the initiating impulse of my book *The Forgotten Ways*, which was to answer how they did this. My attempt at an answer to this question has guided the writing of *Right Here, Right Now*. It constitutes some of that reframing that is needed to reinvent ourselves in our time.

But my role is not quite finished. I started with the *briefing*—an attempt to give some positive framework of how the everyday Christian might engage in Jesus' mission more effectively (I don't even use the terms "clergy/laity" because

I believe that lies at the root of many of our problems). And then my slightly zany buddy Lance offered his somewhat folksy all-American twist to what it means to activate your own missional moxie. His story should provide some cultural references that connect with the story of most of our intended readers. In this final chapter, I will do what we can call the *debriefing*. There are some things that just need to be said. So this chapter will involve naming some of the things that I believe must be dealt with if we are going to do the particular tasks God has for us to do at the dawn of the twenty-first century (Eph. 2:10). These are some of the proverbial elephants in the room: the big issues we must face but most people simply dodge because they are considered too hard to deal with.

To chase the elephants from the room, I am going to have to use a stick at the very least. So here you have Hirschy with a stick in his hand. Not me at my nicest, but to heal a system that you deeply love, you sometimes have got to get over being "nice."

## There's Nothing like a Good Stretch

As you will have noticed by now, this book stretches the meaning of what we normally mean by "church." We make no apology for this: there is no doubt that over time, our idea of the church has shrunk to unbiblical proportions—so we need some stretching, as ridiculous as that sounds. Our best thinkers have long recognized that the gospel has been effectively marginalized and Christianity relegated to the realm of private, individualized, religious opinion with little impact on the broader world of politics, science, economics, art, and culture.[1] If ever there was a time to reimagine the church and its mission, it is now.

We certainly need to think of the church more as an exponential *people movement* involving all of God's people and not an institution run by religious professionals offering different brands of religious goods and services. But to stretch our ecclesiology will require that we have to somehow get a handle on the basics of what makes a church, well . . . a *church*. This is because in reinventing the church for the particular challenges of our era, we run the risk of ending up being less of what the Bible means by "church" than before. So we must go back to Scripture to rediscover what theologians have called the "marks" or "identifiers" of the church that Jesus built and start again from there.

In saying this, I am not suggesting it's all bad. But I do think that the traditional marks of the church that stemmed from the Reformation are woefully inadequate to equip the contemporary Western church to deal with the bewildering missionary challenge we face. The traditional marks all orbit around the practice of the sacraments. The Reformers argued about whether it was two, three, or seven (the Catholics), but they all agreed that the church is the place where the sacraments are administered and experienced. The problem with all these formulations, however, is that they effectively "institutionalize" grace by making it something that only the priests can handle, usually in "churchly" contexts. Gone is the idea of a people movement that so characterized the early church. Gone is the idea of a Philip simply baptizing the eunuch, gone are the actual meals in houses that made communion a daily affair. Not to mention that they say nothing about mission, discipleship, and cultural life beyond the confines of the church institution itself. What is clearly inadequate can therefore prove to be culturally oppressive to the so-called laity—those believers who have to exercise their following of Jesus outside of the confines of the church's organizational life. It's time for a stretch, don't you think?

In *The Forgotten Ways* I tell the story of how my own community had to get back to basics to assess if, and how, we were being an authentic and faithful expression of Jesus' church. The outcomes of that inquiry I believe still stack up well in providing us with some working essentials for a New Testament ecclesiology (doctrine of the church).[2] So this is what I believe is a useful (but not the *only*) way of identifying a faithful expression of church.

A church is . . .

- *Centered on Jesus*: He is the new covenant with God and he thus forms the true epicentre of an authentic *Christ*-ian faith. An ecclesia is not just a God-community—there are many such religious communities around. We are defined by our relationship to the Second Person of the Trinity, the Mediator, Jesus Christ. We believe in the Trinity to be sure, but take Jesus out and it simply isn't a church anymore. A community centered on Jesus as Lord participates in the salvation that he brings. We receive the grace of God in him.

- *A covenanted community*: A church is a formed people, and not by people just hanging out together, but ones bound together in a distinctive bond. There is a certain obligation toward one another formed around a covenant. So here a covenant community is a network of relationships formed around Jesus our Lord. Remember this does not imply buildings per se.

But, more is required to truly constitute a church. Let me suggest that a true encounter with God in Jesus must result in . . .

- *Worship*: defined as offering our lives back to God through Jesus. Note that this is an all-of-life, biblically stretched definition. It includes communal praise and learning, but extends to every aspect of a life and a world offered back to God in worship.

- *Discipleship*: defined as following Jesus and becoming increasingly like him (Christlikeness). Again, this is not just "church" as we tend to define it. It's the relational fabric of the church that reaches way beyond organizational boundaries.

- *Mission*: defined as extending the mission (the redemptive purposes) of God through the activities of his people in every sphere and domain of life, including, of course, church planting but not confined to it.

So there are five identifiers, or marks, in the above model. Graphically it might look something like this:

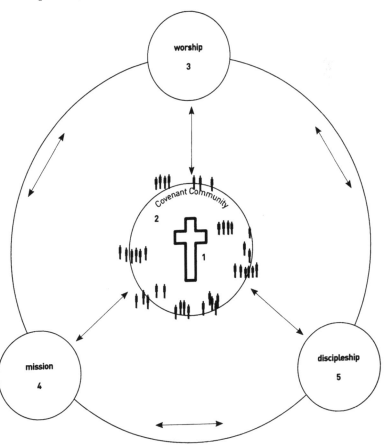

We can easily see that these are profoundly interlinked and inform each other to create a complex phenomenon that constitutes the basics of church as Jesus intended. They describe the core (minimal?) aspects of a faithful *ecclesia*. If some are really missing, or are significantly diminished, we should be asking some serious questions about ourselves.

## Filling the Gaps

Another absolutely central issue we face in a world that is largely turning away from Christianity is that we have to reestablish credibility. That people all across America (and the Western world for that matter) think that *Christ*-ians are fundamentally *unlike* Christ is a serious problem! And research is clear on this trend;[3] as we have seen, most people in the various neighborhoods and contexts we inhabit are actually very open to God, Jesus, and spirituality and are willing to engage in meaningful dialogue around these topics. What they manifestly *are not* open to is "the church." That means the basics of our message are intact; but the medium of the message, the messengers so to speak, are excluded from the equation. And while "the church" is always an easy target and often gets unjustly bad press, this should give us pause to think seriously about what we are currently doing that gives the impression it seems to be giving.

Credibility is a major source of currency for any organization, but especially for the church that Jesus built, and its loss will almost definitely result in a proportionate loss of missional influence on those around about us. Let's face it, if we are not fundamentally different from anyone else (and statistics indicate that this is the case in almost every sphere of morality: money, sex, and power), then why would anyone want to take on the "yoke" of the kingdom of God? If the gospel with all its demands of living under a Lord doesn't seem to have any transformative effect on its messengers, why believe the Message?

Without deemphasizing the contribution of the great missionaries like Paul, seminal sociologist of religion Rodney Stark in his various books maintains that the greatest factor in the growth of early Christianity was the example of ordinary Christians living out their faith in their communities.[4] In fact, he documents the fact that Christianity grew substantially at the time of the terrible plagues that swept the Roman Empire in the first few centuries; there were massive spikes in the growth of the church around these times. The reason for these growth spurts, he suggests, was because while all the pagans abandoned their sick and ran to the hills, the Christians stayed behind to care for the sick and many of them died in this sacrificial service. But many of the sick survived to tell the tale, and tell it they did. The sheer mercy and goodness of the ordinary, marginalized Christians stunned the pagan peoples of that time because such Christlike compassion and service was unknown to them. It was the sheer *goodness* of the Christian church that established the moral credibility of its message and laid the grounds for the spiritual transformation of the Roman Empire. The early church did not seem to have the credibility gap that we so struggle with. *The medium was the message!* Jesus was alive and real in, and to, the people.

As far as I can discern, the only way for Christians to overcome our credibility gap, after centuries of Christianity, is by reactivating an authentic discipleship. Why? Because at its core, discipleship is becoming more like Jesus, or as I tag it in *The Forgotten Ways*, "becoming a little Jesus." God knows, the world certainly doesn't need more "religion"; but it can certainly do with a whole lot more Jesus-like people around the place. One of the key roles of Jesus in the life and imagination of believers is to provide a model for our own humanity. Jesus as Man is the prototypal humanity as God defines it. Ask yourself the question, how bad will I be if I became more and more like Jesus, the most perfect human who ever lived? And this is why getting back to the basics of discipleship is so essential to the mission of the church—it's about establishing Christ's presence everywhere through our lives as his people *right here, right now*, through the very medium of a life well lived. If we miss *this* . . . well, then surely it doesn't really matter what we do elsewhere. In fact, as stated in *Untamed* and *reJesus*, if we just simply get more "religious" and moralistic, then we are likely to do more damage than good.[5]

## All-Consuming Fires

The overwhelming economic and social environment in which we are raised in the West profoundly impacts us all. We are all born into a culture that gets to shape us—in fact, *disciple* us—from the time of birth to death. The truth is that Western culture at the dawn of the twenty-first century is a particularly potent culture because of the omnipresent pervasiveness of media and the predominant role of market forces (with associated money and consumption) in our lives. We have to simply assume that the prevalent values and perspectives of the culture are being downloaded into each one of us from an early age; some of them are clearly good, some of them not so much.

The problem with these cultural ideas is that we generally can't "see" them. Culture is invisible to those immersed in it; it's like asking the proverbial fish to define water. We assume its rightness until we are confronted with an alternative vision of reality that calls it into question. It takes a fair bit of self-reflection, and I would say a very proactive, untamed discipleship in the Way of Jesus, to discern the darker sides of the culture. This is why the kingdom of God can only be experienced as a conversion from one system (kingdom) into another (e.g., Col. 1:13; 1 Thess. 1:9).

The point of this unnerving piece of information is that we simply have to be more aware of our own largely middle-class, and profoundly consumerist, biases if we are going to be effective missional agents in our time. Once again, it's not that being middle-class is wrong per se; it's just that it has *some* values that are consistent with the kingdom of God, but make no mistake, it has others that work to undermine Jesus' mission and purpose in the world.[6] Obsession with personal security or the desire for increasing amounts of money and power are problematic when dealing with the Lord Jesus. Even something as seemingly right as "getting an education" can become an idol that is designed to secure ourselves and resist God's will for our lives—and let me be clear here, I am *not* saying that education is wrong, far from it, but just like all things, it can become a means of disobedience and rebellion. *Education is real social power and capital*, and the fact is, we middle-class folk use it all the time; it's unlikely to be spiritually neutral.

Likewise with consumerism; to buy things is basic to survival in a market-based economy like ours, but *to be defined by what we buy* is another thing altogether. The truth is that marketing exploits our deepest fears and desires in order to sell products. They have to. The factories and the economy produce much, much more than we *need*, so in order to keep the system operative, to make the capital work on its own terms, we have to keep the fires of consumption burning. To do this, marketing has to *create desire* and then seek to fulfill it through the purchasing of products. I am not being snide, cynical, or anticapitalist here, so please don't dismiss what is being said for reasons of defensiveness. This is patently the case; consider how much of what you buy today will still be used by you in six months' time. Research says that only 5 to 10 percent will still be in use in six months; the rest is either thrown out into the garbage or becomes someone else's product—mostly thrown out.[7] Track what happens to the Christmas toys you buy for the kids, or last season's fashions, to make the point.

Heck, we all go into debt to buy things we don't really need. Ever asked why? What's really driving us? Well, the aim is to create need in order to keep the factories, and therefore the economy, firing. But this takes a significantly spiritual twist in our own day—because in a more and more competitive environment, marketers have to reach deeper and deeper into human motivation to be able to sell us things we don't really need. There is no doubt that when we go shopping, something akin to spirituality is at work. We buy not just to live and survive but also to fulfill a search for meaning, identity, purpose, and belonging. And here is where consumerism clashes with the claims of the kingdom.

And why is all this important? Well, apart from the serious implications for discipleship, global justice, and the environment, because it's our culture, and as we saw in the briefing, sometimes in order to be faithful agents of the King, we simply have to subvert it. Also, we need to demonstrate, witness to, a more righteous way of life. The fact is that all the consumption and the relative wealth of people in the West has not made us happy at all. Depression and suicide are largely problems in Western cultural contexts. The children in America are more likely to kill themselves than those in a Brazilian slum! This has to say something to us. It's a big elephant in the room and it has to be confronted if we are going to be missional Christians *right here, right now.*

## — Suggestions for Further Reflection —

- To explore the various hindrances that keep us from being revolutionary disciples, read Alan Hirsch and Debra Hirsch, *Untamed.*
- Watch Mark Sayers's stimulating video (with book and study guide) *The Trouble with Paris* with a group of people and discuss.
- View and discuss the online video *The Story of Stuff* (www.storyofstuff.com).

- For implications of consumerism on Christian spirituality, read Skye Jethani, *The Divine Commodity: Discovering a Faith Beyond Consumer Christianity.*
- For Christian authenticity in the suburbs, explore books by Albert Y. Hsu, *The Suburban Christian: Finding Spiritual Vitality in the Land of Plenty*, and Dave L. Goetz, *Death by Suburb: How to Keep the Suburbs from Killing Your Soul.*

## Kingdom City Limits?

Here's a biggie, and one most believers seldom, if ever, stop to think about even in a lifetime. It goes something like this: we tend to so completely identify the church with the kingdom of God that we end up with what we might call *ecclesiocrasy* (rule by the church). And if this sounds like a rather absurd notion (that the clergy once ruled the world), be assured that it has dominated European understandings of the church for a long, long time. In fact, this dangerous error of category lies at the root of false ideas of the church. For instance, when the Roman Catholic Church talks about the pope as Christ's vicar, they mean that he is Jesus' sole, authoritative representative, and that Christ rules his world through the medium of the church, of which the pope is the unquestioned boss! I kid you not. As far as I am aware, this basic understanding of the doctrine of the church is still held by the Catholic Church.[8]

But we all continue to get the distinction between kingdom and church very wrong, and with disastrous consequences. Let me suggest that the basic mistake here is to make a complete correlation of the church—the redeemed community of Jesus' people—with God's kingdom—his active government or rule in the world.

Is the kingdom of God simply to be equated with the church? I sincerely hope not. As much as I love the church and believe that it is a nonnegotiable part of God's plan, it is to King Jesus and not any human agency that I must give my ultimate allegiance. The church is not simply the same as the kingdom. The church is an expression of the kingdom, perhaps even the most consistent expression of it, but the kingdom (God's active rule in and over his universe) is *much* larger than the church—in fact, it is cosmic in scope.

Reggie McNeal wisely suggests that we need a kingdom-shaped view of the church, not a church-shaped view of the kingdom. In other words, as God's people we must always assess ourselves in the light of God's active rule in the world and not the other way around. Theologian Richard Neuhaus is right when he says,

> Our restless discontent should not be over the distance between ourselves and the first century Church but over the distance between ourselves and the Kingdom of God to which the Church then and now is the witness.[9]

Why all this church-kingdom stuff? Well, because if we are to be effective agents of God's kingdom in this world, we need to be freed to see his kingdom express itself everywhere and anyplace—as indeed it does. God turns up in places where we might least expect to see him, but we need the *eyes* to see what he is doing if we are going to join him in the redemption of the world. A complete association of the kingdom with the church locks up God's activity and links it exclusively to organized church activities like Sunday school, communal worship services, and the like. And as wonderful and necessary as these are to Christian community, the diminished view of the kingdom that results from this will never get us beyond the four walls of the church so that we might fulfill our mission of discipling the nations.

The kingdom of God can't be institutionalized in this way. To the contrary, it challenges all these idolatrous attempts to control it—be it churchly and otherwise! Besides, it's not about simply getting more church-based services up to scratch; it is going to take the *whole body of Christ* as a fluid, dynamic, witnessing agency, active in every possible arena of life, to bring the gospel of God's love into his world. This, in fact, goes to the heart of our mission in the world.

### — SUGGESTIONS FOR FURTHER REFLECTION —

- John Wimber, *The Cost of Commitment*, DVD
- Jim Peterson, *Church without Walls: Moving Beyond Traditional Boundaries*

## Attractional-Extractional

Another elephant in the room is the whole issue of what has come to be called the attractional versus missional church debate. As someone responsible for helping introduce the term into common parlance, let me try to explain it. When we use the term *attractional*, it is an attempt to describe how we conceive of our church in relation to our culture. In other words, it describes our missionary stance or the expectations we have about the role that church plays in our contexts.

To grasp the importance of this, consider the idea of cultural distance.[10] This is a conceptual tool that we can use to discern just how far a person or a people group is from a *meaningful* engagement with the gospel. In order to determine this, we have to see it on a scale that goes something like this:

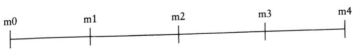

Each numeral with the prefix *m* indicates *one significant cultural barrier to the meaningful communication of the gospel*. An obvious example of such a barrier would be language. All would agree that if you have to reach across a language barrier, you have got a problem and it's going to take some time to communicate *meaningfully*. But others could be race, history, religion/worldview, culture, etc. The more boundaries one has to cross, the harder meaningful communication will be. So for instance, in Islamic contexts, the gospel has struggled to make any significant inroads because religion, race, and a whole lot of *history* make a meaningful engagement with the gospel very difficult indeed. But this is not limited to overseas missions; it is directly related to missionality right here, right now.

Let me bring it closer to home by applying it to the various spheres in which we have to live. If you see yourself (or your church for that matter) standing on the m0 point above, this is how we *might* interpret our own context(s):

| | |
|---|---|
| m0–m1 | Those with some concept of Christianity who speak the same language, have similar interests, probably the same nationality, and are from a similar class grouping as you or your church. Most of your friends would probably fit into this bracket. |
| m1–m2 | Here we go to the average non-Christian in our context: a person who has little real awareness of, or interest in, Christianity but is suspicious about the church (they have heard bad things). These people might be politically correct, socially aware, and open to spirituality. This category might also include those previously offended by a bad experience of church or Christians—some call them "bruised fruit" and they are hard to reach. Just go to the average local pub/bar or nightclub to encounter these people. |
| m2–m3 | People in this group probably have no idea about Christianity. Or they might be part of some ethnic group with different religious impulses or some fringy subculture. This category might also include people marginalized by conservative Christianity—e.g., the gay community. But m2–m3ers are also likely to describe people actively antagonistic toward Christianity as they understand it. E.g., the new atheists. |
| m3–m4 | This group might be inhabited by ethnic and religious groupings with a bad history of the church—e.g., Muslims or Jews. The fact that they are in the West might ameliorate some of the distance, but just about everything else gets in the way of a meaningful dialogue. They are highly resistant to the gospel. Or they are people of completely different language, experience, and worldview. Some immigrant/refugee communities might fit here. |

We are all deeply scripted to believe that we must bring people to our church, and so we seldom take into account the cultural dynamics inherent in that equation. But it's *all about culture*. Our church has a distinct culture, as do the people we are hoping to reach! In fact, as we saw in the briefing, I believe we have come to a situation where all mission in Western settings now should be considered a cross-cultural enterprise.

And remember the obstinate little truth that it is *we* who are the "sent" people of God, and whatever that means to our identity as God's people, it must also sometimes mean *we* must *go* to where the people are. If we fail to "go" to the people, then to encounter the gospel meaningfully they must "come." This is the inbuilt assumption of the attractional church; and it requires that the nonbeliever do all the cross-cultural work to find Jesus, and not us! Make no mistake: for many people, coming to church involves some serious cross-cultural work for them. They have to be the missionaries!

Another very important fact must be remembered here. We know from now old research that within three to five years of a person becoming a Christian, they will have no meaningful relationships with anyone outside the church. So, assuming that we bring them to our church, and we happen to do a good job at it and effectively socialize them into our church community, we are in effect snapping the natural, organic connections that they have with the host community they come from. This is very problematic because we know that the gospel travels along relational lines. Sever the relationships and we effectively stop the outward movement of the gospel into the broader culture. In other words, *attractional evangelism in missionary contexts results in extracting them* from their previous relationships and cultural context. This is a big no-no if we are serious about initiating movements right here, right now.

And this is not to say that churches should not gather. Of course we should—churches are worshiping communities.

Nor is it saying we should not be thoroughly *attractive* when we do. We should be as culturally spicy as we possibly can be. It simply means that when engaging people in m1–m4 distance from us, we should gather *incarnationally* within a host culture/community and not necessarily extract people from their cultural tribe(s) into our church tribe.

Attractional forms of church in missionary contexts eventually are self-defeating because the church quickly exhausts its supply of relationships and because the new converts quickly become a cultural clique or religious ghetto increasingly marginalized from the original culture.

## Sustainability

Over many years of being involved in missional expressions of church, I perceive one of the biggest issues facing the movement as a whole is that of sustainability. Tragically, many wonderful, spunky people start out with all the right ideas only to end up exhausted and marginalized because they have simply become, well . . . unsustainable.

Part of the issue many disciples face is that of lifestyle and the cultural expectations associated with life in the suburbs—no small matter and one that should be reflected on under the rubric of discipleship. For most believers, the idea of missional discipleship seems like a far-off dream because they work most of the time, come home exhausted, spend what little spare time they have with family and kids, and don't seem to have any time for anything else. Now I don't mean to diminish the sacredness of work and family, but if work is too demanding for us to involve ourselves in being authentic disciples in realms other than work, it is the dominance of our work that should be questioned and not the viability of our discipleship. Work like this is more of an enslaving thing than it is a means of living. We can all live with a lot less. Work four days a week instead of five, if only to find more space for God in your life, let alone serve others. Much real life, relationships, and spiritual meaning can be added by simplifying our lives in order to engage more fully in Life.

Another aspect of unsustainability is the loner mentality that goes along with American individualism. Clearly there are times when one cannot avoid being something of a lone ranger, but we have to learn to see this as the exception that only proves the rule. Jesus always intended that we should seek to engage in mission two by two *at the very least* (Luke 10). Not all of us will be involved in establishing new communities of faith (what I called in the briefing, *apostolic* mission), but all of us ought to be involved in community life in one way or another. And mission in the Way of Jesus should always aim at developing communities of Jesus followers—isn't that what Jesus did? Paul? Other heroes of faith?

In terms of sustainable multiplication church planting associated with people movements, I have always felt that a group of about 30 to 120 has a much greater chance of survival than the smaller cell-group size. Mike Breen, a deeply apostolic friend of mine, rightly notes that this is because what he calls "midsize communities" have their own in-built ecology of survival, especially when each person in the group really looks after the other and is mutually involved in worship, play, economics, and life together. He says we are "hardwired for extended family." We simply don't flourish in the smaller, more nuclear, versions of family, and we are depersonalized in the much larger "tribal" gatherings.[11] Not too big to be unwieldy and mechanical, not too small to seem closed and distressed—that is the trick. But the genius of this lies in the fact that it is church that nonprofessionals can handle and therefore anyone can do. And it's the basis of sustainability.

But a movement that can change the world has to be larger than a local midsized community. I believe strongly in the power of networks and networking.[12] Networks are the fabric of movements and are formed by relationships and mutuality beyond the local expression of church or mission. Through a network, we become a working part of the whole of what God is doing in a city—part of something bigger. It's being part of a *movement*. These networks should be sought after and developed. Depending on where one is starting, as a brand-new pioneering project or an essential, innovative part of an existing church, it is important to seek connection to like-minded established churches, organizations, and networks. The trick is to find a balance of interdependence and not to be dominated by the agenda of some centralist organization. Networks exist on synergistic, win-win relationships through-out the system. Therefore identify and associate with those who understand and practice this.

The other key area of sustainability is the area of finances. Many of the readers of this book will not be church-based professionals and are already involved in "regular jobs" what-ever that might mean. Much is to be gained by looking at the idea of business as mission (BAM). BAM approaches don't accept the dualism that separates the secular from the sacred and sees that all of life can, and indeed must, be made sacred by engaging it in Jesus' name . . . including business. The businesses most likely to engage people personally are obviously the best ways to engage missionally (cafés, Laundromats, coaching, HR, etc.), but even less people-oriented businesses (e.g., engineering firms) have employees who are not disciples of Jesus. These businesses provide a wonderful opportunity for God's kingdom to express itself through his people. In the hands of a missional Christian, the business can become a wonderful tool in the kingdom of God.

In terms of forms of support, in *The Shaping of Things to Come* we suggest that financial support could also come in the following ways:

- Personal support/sponsors: imagine for instance forty people giving $1/day to your support—most of us can get that form of support together.

- Working part-time: great way of modeling what we are asking others to do while engaging non-Christians and keeping our nonchurch skills up.
- From the established church: if what you are doing can be envisioned as part of the broader mission of the local church, then it is not too much to ask for (and expect) a budget allocation.
- Social entrepreneurialism and BAM as described above.
- Mixture of all of the above.

## — SUGGESTIONS FOR FURTHER REFLECTION —

- Alan Hirsch and Michael Frost, *The Shaping of Things to Come*
- Bob Hopkins and Mike Breen, *Clusters: Creative Mid-sized Missional Communities* (London: ACPI, 2008), or visit http://www.3dministries.com/
- Michael Baer, *Business as Mission: The Power of Business in the Kingdom of God*
- Steven Rundle and Tom Steffen, *Great Commission Companies: The Emerging Role of Business in Missions*

### Getting Over Risk Aversion

By and large the church as we know it tends to embody a culture of social restraint and risk aversion. We do not tend to think of "church" as a place where we are likely to experience life-defying adventure . . . or any at all for that matter. Now clearly there is a role for creating a safe environment to raise children and to worship, but when our need for safety overwhelms our vision of a better world, and stifles our sense of obligation to this mission, then there is a need for a serious rethink. The church that Jesus built should be a place of learning and adventurous discipleship. And these by definition must involve to some degree the willingness to experiment, to take risks with people, to venture out into the world in order to change it.

The truth is, *mission is risky*. It involves putting ourselves out of our comfort zones and dealing with people we ordinarily might not engage with. And far from being bad for us, taking risks is actually good for the soul, necessary to a healthy learning process, and vital for innovation in all social contexts. Risk aversion, when it becomes part of the culture of church, will result in a stifling status quo that will resist anything, including God, which comes along to disturb it. We do well to consider that Jesus is always "dangerous" to our all-too-human penchant for safety and security. He is a Lord, how else could it be otherwise?

## — Suggestions for Further Reflection —

- Alan Hirsch and Michael Frost, *The Faith of Leap: A Theology of Adventure and Risk and the Implications for Discipleship, Mission, Leadership, & the Church*[13]
- Alan Hirsch, *The Forgotten Ways*, chap. 8
- Watch several adventure movies and ask what makes them so appealing to the human spirit.

This chapter is filled with both a sense of urgency and a sense of desperation. Urgency, because it's hard to dodge the fact that the twenty-first century presents a major challenge to Christianity as we currently know it. Think about any science fiction movie of significance. Is there any mention at all in them of even the possibility of Christian faith? I certainly cannot recall any. And remember, science fiction, as a literary genre, is about human imagination exploring the possibilities of the future . . . whether they be nightmarish or utopian. The fact that the church is missing from the genre means that it plays no significant role in the imagination of what the future holds. It's seen as irrelevant to the great issues of our day—people are not looking in our direction to lead them into the future . . . and yet who better to do that very thing?

Henri Nouwen underscored the perception of those outside the church as he told the story of serving as a chaplain of a cruise ship that was navigating a dangerous fog. "The captain, carefully listening to a radar station operator who was explaining his position between other ships, walked nervously up and down the bridge and shouted his orders to the steersman." When he suddenly stumbled over Nouwen, he blurted out what a lot of people think about the church and its ministry: "God damn it, Father, get out of my way." When it came down to navigating the ship out of danger, Nouwen felt totally useless and unwanted—it seemed that chaplains are only called in to life out of a sense of an obligatory tip of the hat to religion.[14]

The reality is, we have been pushed from the places where it really matters. Even if we can project ourselves onto the end of the twenty-first century, what will we see there in terms of viable Christian faith? To be honest, I find it very hard to see the privatized, institution-based religion that we experience now surviving into any of these futures—at least as a significant social force for good. That is, *unless* we adapt. It's all there in the "unless"—the possibility of repentance and change.

I believe with every inch of my soul that the church that Jesus built, when it is authentic and true, is by far and away the most powerful force for the transformation of the world. The gospel will always be the good news of God that always addresses the human situation. But the church as we know it is going to have to become more aligned with it, more relevant in all spheres of life, more missional right here, right now, if it is going to effectively deliver its Message to the end of this, what will prove to be an extremely challenging, century.

The desperation I feel stems from knowing that we have a great opportunity right here, right now to recalibrate ourselves for what is coming. In fact, I believe that this recalibration, this rebooting, is well under way. We can, and I believe *will*, become a people movement again. But only if we can awaken both sides of the movement equation as discussed in the briefing. We need the *apostolic mission* to engage in exponential church planting, creating communities of faith wherever and whenever we can—many of them, and much more diverse than what we now experience. But the other side is also vitally important. We need to awaken the sheer missional moxie of God's people as a whole. And we all need to recognize and live out the reality that we are all commissioned (dare I say, *ordained*) agents of the King, and we live out that agency in every sphere and domain of society. Everyone gets to play! If we fail to awaken the sleeping giant of the body of Christ, then I believe our opportunity will be lost and the church will continue to decline, and eventually become a mere cultural footnote to Western history.

Much depends on our choices and actions now. I dream that some brothers and sisters, standing at the dawn of the next century, will look back to our time and say that the course of history was changed because many of us broke from the herd and under God rediscovered our courage, along with the missional potentials that lie dormant in God's people.

> All of us dream, but not equally.
> Those who dream by night,
> in the dusty recesses of their minds,
> wake in the day to find that it was vanity.
> But the dreamers of the day are dangerous folk,
> for they may act their dreams with open eyes
> to make it possible.
>
> —T. E. Lawrence ("Lawrence of Arabia"),
> *The Seven Pillars of Wisdom*

# NOTES

## Introduction

1. Alan Hirsch and Debra Hirsch, *Untamed: Reactivating a Missional Form of Discipleship* (Grand Rapids: Baker, 2010).

2. Alan Hirsch and Michael Frost, *The Shaping of Things to Come: Mission and Innovation for the 21ˢᵗ-Century Church* (Peabody, MA: Hendrickson, 2003).

3. Alan Hirsch with Darryn Altclass, *The Forgotten Ways Handbook: A Practical Guide for Developing Missional Churches* (Grand Rapids: Brazos, 2009).

4. Alan Hirsch, *The Forgotten Ways: Reactivating the Missional Church* (Grand Rapids: Brazos, 2008).

5. Michael Frost and Alan Hirsch, *ReJesus: A Wild Messiah for a Missional Church* (Peabody, MA: Hendrickson, 2009).

6. Hugh Halter and Matt Smay, *The Tangible Kingdom: Creating Incarnational Community* (San Francisco: Jossey Bass, 2008); and Smay and Halter, *The Tangible Kingdom Primer: An Eight-Week Guide to Incarnational Community* (Anaheim: CRM, 2009).

7. Michael Frost, *Exiles: Living Missionally in a Post-Christian Culture* (Peabody, MA: Hendrickson, 2006).

## Briefing

1. Hirsch, *Forgotten Ways*, 114.

2. From notes at http://www.seobook.com/review-seth-godins-tribes.

3. http://zenhabits.net/2009/05/the-art-of-the-small-how-to-make-an-impact/.

4. Read the Tom's Shoes story at http://www.tomsshoes.com/content.asp?tid=227.
Read the Laundry Love story at http://laundrylovesantaana.com/about/.

5. Much of what follows is taken from an article by Keller on Missional Church found here: http://www.pdfdownload.org/pdf2html/pdf2html.php?url=http%3A%2F%2Fwww.redeemer2.com%2Fresources%2Fpapers%2Fmissional.pdf&images=yes.

6. Ibid.

7. Mark Van Steenwyk, "Incarnational Practices," *NextWave*, http://www.the-next-wave-ezine.info/issue82/index.cfm?id=5&ref=COVERSTORY.

8. Hirsch, *Forgotten Ways*, 95–97.

9. Van Steenwyk, "Incarnational Practices."

10. Hirsch, *Forgotten Ways Handbook*, 92–97.

11. Tim Keller, The Missional Church, June 2001, http://www.pdfdownload.org/pdf2html/pdf2html.php?url=http%3A%2F%2Fwww.redeemer2.com%2Fresources%2Fpapers%2Fmissional.pdf&images=yes.

12. Hirsch and Hirsch, *Untamed*. We suggest that the reader explore what is said there in relation to pre-conversion and post-conversion discipleship.

13. Hirsch, *Forgotten Ways*, 211ff.

14. Addison notes that preexisting relationships are a critical factor for the exponential growth of a movement. "New religious movements fail when they become closed or semi-closed networks. For continued exponential growth, a movement must maintain open relationships with outsiders. They must reach out into new, adjacent social networks." Stephen Addison, "Movement Dynamics: Keys to the Expansion and Renewal of the Church in Mission" (unpublished manuscript, 2003), 52. Stark argues that as movements grow, their "social surface" expands exponentially. Each new member opens up new networks of relationships between the movement and potential members—provided the movement continues to remain an open system. The forms of social networks will differ from culture to culture, but "however people constitute structures of direct interpersonal attachments, those structures will define the lines through which conversion will most readily proceed." Rodney Stark, *The Rise of Christianity: How the Obscure, Marginal, Jesus Movement Became the Dominant Religious Force in the Western World in a Few Centuries* (San Francisco: HarperCollins, 1996), 22.

15. For an excellent exploration into the power of networking, see Dwight Friesen, *Thy Kingdom Connected: What the Church Can Learn from Facebook, the Internet, and Other Networks* (Grand Rapids: Baker, 2009); or Neil Cole's *Church 3.0: Upgrades for the Future of the Church* (San Francisco: Jossey-Bass, 2010).

16. Hirsch and Frost, *Shaping of Things to Come*, 100.

17. See *Untamed*, section 2, to explore ways in which we as disciples must challenge prevailing views of culture and *The Shaping of Things to Come*, chap. 9, to explore how and why the medium is the message.

18. Compiled from Keller, Missional Church.

19. Hirsch, *Forgotten Ways*, 17.

20. Keller, Missional Church.

## Chapter 1 Putting the Extra in the Ordinary

1. Hirsch, *Forgotten Ways*, 130.

2. Hirsch and Hirsch, *Untamed*, 95.

3. Craig Van Gelder, ed., *Confident Witness—Changing World: Rediscovering the Gospel in North America* (Grand Rapids: Eerdmans, 1999), 115.

4. "This is another word for Christendom, because Christendom was basically initiated by Constantine's actions in bringing the church into official relationship

with the state. Constantinianism is the type of all modes of church that resulted from the merger between church and state and has dominated our mindsets for the last seventeen centuries." From the glossary in Alan's book, *Forgotten Ways*, 278.

5. Rodney Clapp, *A Peculiar People* (Downers Grove, IL: InterVarsity, 1996), 23.

6. *The Epistle of Mathetes to Diognetus*, chap. 5, http://www.earlychristian writings.com/text/diognetus-roberts.html.

7. Dallas Willard, *The Divine Conspiracy* (San Francisco: HarperCollins, 1998), 20.

8. George Ladd, *A Theology of the New Testament* (San Francisco: Harper-Collins, 1998), 20.

## Chapter 2 Meet the Extras

1. Randy Frazee, *The Connecting Church* (Grand Rapids: Zondervan, 2001), 115.

2. Frost and Hirsch, *ReJesus*, 34.

3. First Impressions Are All in the Brain, http://www.webmd.com/brain/news/20090306/first-impressions-are-all-in-the-brain.

4. Ibid.

5. Carlin Flora, "The First Impression," *Psychology Today*, May 14, 2004, http://www.psychologytoday.com/node/21934.

6. Greek lexicon based on Thayer's and Smith's *Bible Dictionary* plus others; this is keyed to the large Kittel and the *Theological Dictionary of the New Testament*. These files are public domain.

7. Peter Senge, *The Fifth Discipline Fieldbook* (New York: Doubleday, 1994), 3.

8. Michael Schluter and David Lee, *The R Factor* (London: Hodder & Stoughton, 1993), 10.

9. Ibid., 13.

10. Brennan Manning, *The Wisdom of Tenderness* (San Francisco: Harper-Collins, 2002), 76–77.

11. "Why It Is Hard to Keep a Straight Face," BBC News, October 22, 2002, http://news.bbc.co.uk/2/hi/science/nature/2349981.stm.

12. Todd Hunter, *Christianity Beyond Belief: Following Jesus for the Sake of Others* (San Francisco: HarperCollins, 2002), 114–17.

13. Ibid.

## Chapter 3 From Paper to Pavement

1. Willard, *Divine Conspiracy*, 283.

2. Frost and Hirsch, *ReJesus*, 149.

3. Lesslie Newbigin, *Truth to Tell: The Gospel as Public Truth* (Grand Rapids: Eerdmans, 1991), 28.

4. Brennan Manning, *The Signature of Jesus* (Sisters, OR: Multnomah, 1996), 33.

5. Neil Brower, *Mayberry 101* (Winston Salem, NC: John F. Blair Publishing, 1998), 53.

6. Johann Metz, *The Emergent Church* (New York: Crossroad, 1981), 3.
7. Manning, *Signature of Jesus*, 57.
8. Robert Webber, *Ancient-Future Faith* (Grand Rapids: Baker, 1999), 45.
9. Dietrich Bonhoeffer, *The Cost of Discipleship* (New York: Simon & Schuster, 1995), 62–63.
10. Hirsch and Frost, *Shaping of Things to Come*, 120.

## Chapter 4 Laodicean Cul-de-sacs

1. John Paul II, "Respect for Human Rights: The Secret of True Peace," message for 1999 World Day of Peace.
2. David Meyers, *The American Paradox* (New Haven: Yale University Press, 2000), 136.
3. Peter Whybrow, *American Mania: When More Is Not Enough* (New York: W. W. Norton, 2005), 3.
4. Justo González, *Faith and Wealth: A History of Early Christian Ideas on the Origin, Significance, and Use of Money* (San Francisco: HarperCollins, 2000), 76.
5. Whybrow, *American Mania*, 38.
6. Vincent Miller, *Consuming Religion* (New York: Continuum, 2005), 49.
7. Ronald Sider, *Rich Christians in an Age of Hunger: Moving from Affluence to Generosity* (Dallas: Word, 1997), 97.
8. Miller, *Consuming Religion*, 119.

## Chapter 5 Losing for Winning

1. Miller, *Consuming Religion*, 132.
2. Philip Olson, Ronald Sider, and Heidi Unruh, *Churches That Make a Difference* (Grand Rapids: Baker, 2002), 50.
3. John de Graff, *Affluenza* (San Francisco: Berrett-Koehler, 2001), 24.
4. Van Gelder, *Confident Witness*, 139.
5. List excerpted from ibid., 140.
6. http://www.cnn.com/2009/LIVING/personal/02/19/survivor.extendedfamily/index.html.
7. Scott Bessenecker, *How to Inherit the Earth* (Downers Grove, IL: InterVarsity, 2009), 72–73.

## Chapter 6 Oh Raaaawb!

1. Philip Langdon, *A Better Place to Live: Reshaping the American Suburb* (Amherst, MA: University of Massachusetts Press, 1994), 31.
2. David Halpern, *Social Capitol* (Cambridge, UK: Polity Press, 2005), 2.
3. Peter Block, *Community* (San Francisco: Berrett-Koehler, 2008), 17.
4. Stephanie Coontz, *The Way We Never Were* (New York: Basic Books, 2000), 17.
5. Ibid., 24.
6. Ibid., 27.
7. Langdon, *Better Place to Live*, 3.
8. Coontz, *Way We Never Were*, 15.

9. Langdon, *Better Place to Live*, 44.

10. Pratt and Brody, Depression in the United States Household Population, 2005–2006, http://www.cdc.gov/nchs/data/databriefs/db07.htm.

11. Deepa Babington, "Americans Less Happy Today than 30 Years Ago: Study," June 15, 2007, http://www.reuters.com/article/lifestyleMolt/idUSL1550309820070615.

12. Coontz, *Way We Never Were*, 45.

13. Dan Chiras and Dave Wann, *Superbia* (Gabriola Island, BC: New Society Publishers, 2003), 90.

## Chapter 7 Beyond Kumbaya

1. Norman Kraus, *The Community of the Spirit* (Scottdale, PA: Herald Press, 1993), 170.

2. Gonzáles, *Faith and Wealth*, 83.

3. 2 Corinthians 6:6 KJV.

4. 1 Peter 1:22 KJV.

5. Francis Schaeffer, *The Mark of the Christian* (London: Norfolk Press, 1970), 16.

6. Frost, *Exiles*, 150.

7. Henri Nouwen, *Reaching Out* (New York: Doubleday, 1975), 52.

## Chapter 8 Y'all Come Back Now, Ya Hear?

1. Dorothy Bass, *Practicing Our Faith* (San Francisco: Josey-Bass, 1997), 3.

2. Mike McIntyre, *The Kindness of Strangers* (New York: Berkley Books, 1996), 42, 51, 183.

3. Nouwen, *Reaching Out*, 66.

4. Ibid.

5. Christine Pohl, *Making Room* (Grand Rapids: Eerdmans, 1999), 4.

6. Bass, *Practicing Our Faith*, 32.

7. Robert Banks, *Paul's Idea of Community* (Peabody, MA: Hendrickson, 1994), 83.

## Chapter 9 Salt Blocks and Salt Shakers

1. Jim Peterson, *Church Without Walls: Moving Beyond Traditional Boundaries* (Colorado Springs: NavPress, 1992), 150.

2. Hirsch, *Forgotten Ways*, 34.

3. Howard Snyder, *Global Good News: Mission in a New Context* (Nashville: Abingdon, 2001), 91.

4. John Hayes, *Sub-merge* (Ventura, CA: Regal, 2006), 181.

5. Written from Aaron Snow to Alan and Lance.

## Debriefing

1. For instance Lesslie Newbigin, *Foolishness to the Greeks: The Gospel and Western Culture* (Grand Rapids: Eerdmans, 1986).

2. Hirsch, *Forgotten Ways*, 40–41.

3. George Barna, *Revolution* (Carol Stream, IL: Tyndale, 2006); Dave Kinnaman and Gabe Lyons, *unChristian: What a New Generation Really Thinks about Christianity . . . and Why It Matters* (Grand Rapids: Baker, 2007); and Dan Kimball's *They Like Jesus but Not the Church* (Grand Rapids: Zondervan, 2007) are just samplings of the research available.

4. Rodney Stark, *Cities of God: The Real Story of How Christianity Became an Urban Movement and Conquered Rome* (New York: HarperCollins, 2006), chap. 1, and *Rise of Christianity,* chaps. 1–3.

5. See Deb's and my book on missional Christianity/discipleship called *Untamed*, especially chapters 1 and 2 on toxic religion and Frost and Hirsch, *reJesus*, on Christianity minus Christ equals Religion, 68ff.

6. Deb and I wrote a whole book about obstructions that get in the way of discipleship. See *Untamed: Reactivating a Missional Form of Discipleship.*

7. See the video "The Story of Stuff" at http://www.storyofstuff.com/.

8. Eminent philosopher Karl Popper traces the basis of this ecclesial structure to Plato's idea of the Republic as the mediating institution between the real world of ideas and the false world of senses. The church assumes the role of mediating agent between God and the people. He, I think rightly, sees it as one vast negative that led to an oppressive authorizing of the institution over the people. See Karl Popper, *The Open Society and Its Enemies: The Spell of Plato,* vol. 1 (New York: Routledge, 2002).

9. Richard J. Neuhaus, *Freedom for Ministry* (Grand Rapids: Eerdmans, 1992), 33.

10. Hirsch, *Forgotten Ways,* 56–57.

11. See their website for great materials at www.3dministries.com.

12. Hirsch, *Forgotten Ways,* chap. 7.

13. Forthcoming (Grand Rapids: Baker, 2011).

14. Henri Nouwen, *The Wounded Healer: Ministry in Contemporary Society* (New York: Doubleday, 1979), 86.

Alan Hirsch is the founding director of Forge Mission Training Network. He is the cofounder of Shapevine.com, an international forum for engaging with world-transforming ideas. Currently he leads an innovative learning program called Future Travelers, helping numerous megachurches become missional movements. He has also been part of the leadership team of Christian Associates, a missional church-planting agency with focus on Western Europe. Known for his innovative approach to mission, Alan is a teacher and key mission strategist for churches across the Western world. His various books are widely considered to be seminal texts on mission, leadership, and ministry. They include, among others, *The Forgotten Ways*, *Untamed*, *ReJesus*, and *The Shaping of Things to Come*.

His experience in leadership includes leading a local church movement among the marginalized, developing training systems for innovative missional leadership, as well as heading up the Mission and Revitalization work of his denomination.

Alan is an adjunct professor at Fuller Seminary, George Fox Evangelical Seminary, and Wheaton College, among others, and lectures frequently throughout Australia, Europe, and the US.

Lance Ford is the cofounder and director of Shapevine.com and the former director of the Northwood Church Multiplication Center. With more than twenty years of experience as a pastor and church planter, Lance is a writer, coach, and consultant who has designed unique training systems currently being used by networks, seminaries, and leaders throughout the world. He is also an adjunct professor at Biblical Seminary in Hatfield, Pennsylvania. Lance serves as a Missional Strategist for the MidAmerica District of The Christian and Missionary Alliance and lives with his wife in Kansas City, Missouri.

# From Missional Expert
# ALAN HIRSCH

+reactivating the missional church

**THE FORGOTTEN WAYS**

ALAN HIRSCH

foreword by leonard sweet

9781587431647

"The global mission community is indebted to Hirsch for this seminal book. It is packed with solid exegesis and theological reflection. . . . There is rich insight in each chapter for field practitioners and a fresh synthesis of the essentials of biblical missiology." —**Steve Hoke**, *Evangelical Missions Quarterly*

ALAN HIRSCH
WITH DARRYN ALTCLASS

**THE FORGOTTEN WAYS HANDBOOK**

+a practical guide for developing missional churches

9781587432491

*The Forgotten Ways Handbook* moves beyond theory to practice, offering ways for any missionally minded person to apply the ideas contained in *The Forgotten Ways* to their life and ministry.

**Brazos Press**
a division of Baker Publishing Group
www.BrazosPress.com

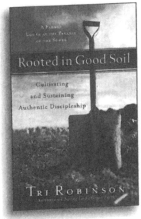

Made in the USA
San Bernardino, CA
23 May 2014